UA

How To **Knit**

How To **Knit**

contributing author **Helen Ardley**

Bounty
BOOKS

First published in Great Britain in 2008 by Hamlyn
a division of Octopus Publishing Group Ltd

This edition published in 2009 by Bounty Books,
a division of Octopus Publishing Group Ltd
2–4 Heron Quays, London E14 4JP
www.octopusbooks.co.uk

An Hachette UK Company
www.hachette.co.uk

Some of the material in this book has previously appeared in *The
Hamlyn Complete Knitters Course*, *The Knitter's Handbook* or in *Easy
Knits*, all published by Hamlyn

Copyright © Octopus Publishing Group Ltd 2003, 2006, 2008

ISBN: 978-0-753719-11-4

A CIP catalogue record for this book is available from the British
Library

Printed and bound in China

A note on buying yarn

Where possible, the yarn brand recommended in the pattern
should be used. If substituting yarn, it is recommended that you
find one of a similar thickness and weight and that you knit a
tension square to check the stitch size and the hang of the fabric.

Yarn is dyed in batches and dye lots can vary greatly. It is essential
to check the dye lot number on the yarn label of all balls of yarn
used for the main colour of the knitted project to make sure they
are from the same dye lot.

It should be noted that yarn manufactures change the colours of
the yarns they produce on a regular basis. If you are unable to find
the exact colours suggested in the patterns in this book, your yarn
supplier should be able to help you find a close match.

Contents

Abbreviations

alt alternate

approx approximate(ly)

beg begin(ning)

cm centimetre(s)

cont continu(e)(ing)

dec decreas(e)(ing)

DK double-knitting-weight yarn

foll follow(s)(ing)

g gram(s)

in inch(es)

inc increas(e)(ing)

K knit

LH left hand

M1 make 1: pick up strand between stitch just worked and next stitch on LH needle and knit into back of it

mm millimetre(s)

oz ounce(s)

P purl

patt pattern *or* work in pattern

psso pass slipped over stitch

rem remain(ing)

rep repeat

RH right hand

RS right side

sl slip

st(s) stitch(es)

st st stocking/stockinette stitch (K on RS rows, P on WS rows)

tbl through back of loop(s)

tog together

WS wrong side

wyb with yarn at back of work

wyf with yarn at front of work

yd yard(s)

yf yarn forward (US **yo**)

yon yarn over needle (US **yo**)

yrn yarn round needle (US **yo**)

Introduction

Knitting has great appeal. There are numerous patterns and yarns to choose from and the techniques, once mastered, are easy. You don't need to set aside a huge amount of space to knit in, nor do you need any expensive or sophisticated equipment. This is a relaxing pastime, and one that you can easily pick up and put down wherever and whenever it suits you.

Newcomers to knitting will find this book the perfect resource. Split into two main sections – techniques and projects – the various chapters offer the beginner a comprehensive introduction to knitting from casting on the first stitch to producing clothes and accessories of the very highest quality. The information is presented clearly and logically, with the knitter's skill level increasing chapter by chapter.

You start at the very beginning with the most basic techniques of casting on, knitting and purling and casting/binding off. Once you have mastered these, it is simply a question of learning to follow a pattern before moving on to more advanced techniques such as knitting special textures (bobbles, cables and loops), knitting in the round, working in more than one colour and adding embellishments (beads, tassels and crocheted edges). You will also find instruction on adding zips, hems and pockets.

By the time you complete the techniques section you will be well versed in all of the steps needed to take on a whole project, and there are plenty of beautiful pieces to choose from in the chapters that follow. Here you will find winter warming clothes for friends and family – from cute baby slippers and a child's rugged hoodie, to gorgeous pullovers, hats, gloves and scarves. There are nursery favourites, including a blanket for a newborn baby and a soft knitted bunny and additional accessories including bags and cushions.

At the end of the book you will find a gallery of swatches, showing exactly how each stitch type looks when knitted – the perfect, instant reference when choosing a pattern of your own.

If you've never knitted before, the idea of transforming a ball of yarn into a beautifully knitted garment may seem daunting, but knitting is actually very easy. This section provides information on yarn types and the simple, inexpensive equipment you need for knitting. It shows you how to master the knit and purl stitches, and how to cast on and cast/bind off. These most basic techniques will provide you with a solid foundation for all your future knitting projects.

The basics

Yarns

The yarn you use contributes to the pleasure of knitting but also to the success of the finished piece. Knitting by hand is a very tactile activity, and a yarn that is both pleasing to touch and appropriate for the project will add to your enjoyment of the work and your pride in finishing a garment. There are many yarns to choose from – not only the classic smooth yarns, which never go out of fashion – but also a dazzling variety of unusual textures and fibres, from glossy silk, to velvety chenille, to chunky bouclé. They offer endless creative possibilities and are one good reason for learning to design your own patterns. Even if you use published patterns, as most beginners do, familiarity with the wide variety of different yarns available will only enhance your experience, making you better able to choose the right yarn time and again.

Fibre content

Yarns are made from many different fibres and combinations of fibres, both natural and synthetic.

Natural fibres

Wool is the traditional favourite among natural fibres. It is warm and relatively lightweight. It also has an elastic quality, which makes it easy to knit and means that, if cared for properly, the finished garment holds its shape. Many wools are now machine washable.

Wool varies considerably in texture, depending on the sheep it comes from and the spinning and finishing methods used. The softest quality is Botany wool, which comes from merino sheep raised in Australia. Lambswool is also very soft, since it comes from the first shearing of the young animals.

Mohair is the fluffy hair of the angora goat. Despite its delicate appearance, it is strong, though not very elastic. Kid mohair is softer than ordinary mohair from the adult animal, and tends to be more expensive. For economy, mohair is often combined with other fibres, such as wool or acrylic.

Angora is the fur of the angora rabbit. It is feather-soft and very expensive. Because it has a tendency to shed, it is not recommended for garments for babies, who might choke on the fibres.

Cashmere comes from the Himalayan goat. An extremely soft and luxurious fibre, it is usually blended with other fibres.

Alpaca is the hair of the llama. It is often added to wool yarns to provide extra softness.

Silk, which is spun from the cocoon of the silkworm, is a luxurious fibre with a strength that belies its softness.

Pure silk yarn normally has a glossy finish and comes in beautifully rich colours. Silk is also found combined with other fibres, including wool and mohair.

Cotton comes from the seed heads of the cotton plant. Cotton yarns are cool and are therefore ideal for summer garments. Although it can be expensive, cotton is generally hard-wearing and good value.

Cotton that has been mercerized is particularly strong and lustrous. The only drawbacks with cotton yarn are its lack of elasticity, which makes it rather difficult to knit with, and its density, which makes it slow to dry after laundering.

Linen is a very strong fibre, taken from the stem of the flax plant. It has a naturally slubbed texture and is often combined with cotton.

Synthetic fibres

Synthetic fibres have many practical advantages over most natural ones; they are strong, lightweight, resistant to moths and, in many cases, machine washable. For these reasons, they are often added to natural fibres.

The main synthetic fibres are **acrylic**, **polyamide**, (including nylon), **polyester** and **viscose** (including rayon). Of these, the most common is acrylic, which is very soft and lightweight. Acrylics are sometimes used to create novel textures that are not achievable with natural fibres. A special category of synthetic is the **metallic fibres**, which are derived from aluminium.

Yarns made of 100 per cent synthetic fibres tend to be less satisfying to use than those made of natural fibres, or that are a natural-synthetic blend. They are less pleasing to the touch, and garments made from them are more likely to lose their shape.

This assortment of yarns gives an idea of the wide variety of textures available.

Loosely spun virgin wool

Cashmere/wool mix

Nylon/acrylic/wool/alpaca mix

Tweed wool

Pure merino wool

Alpaca/wool mix

Pure alpaca

Mohair/silk mix

Pure merino wool

Pure wool

Wool/cotton mix

Pure organic cotton

Tweed wool

Giant bouclé

Bouclé

Silk

Silk/mohair/wool mix

Viscose chenille

Polyamide/viscose/mohair novelty yarn

Nylon/mohair novelty yarn

Angora/wool/nylon mix

Space-dyed wool/polyamide mix

Duo-tone wool

Construction

The character of a yarn is determined not only by its fibre content, but also by the spinning and finishing methods used in its manufacture.

Size

Yarns vary enormously in size, or thickness (also called their 'weight'). The smooth, so-called 'classic' yarns can be broken down into seven general weights: two-ply, three-ply, four-ply, double knitting, Aran-weight, chunky and extra-chunky. There is some variation within these categories, but it is usually possible to substitute one yarn for another as long as it is in the same category.

The word 'ply' is used in two ways. Literally, it means an individual strand of fibre. A ply can be of any thickness; therefore, a yarn consisting of two plies might well be thicker than one containing four. However, some yarns are called 'two-ply', 'three-ply' and 'four-ply' to designate not only a ply construction but also an accepted weight category. Moreover, a textured yarn may also be described in relation to these categories; for example, 'knits as four-ply' means that the yarn (irrespective of its construction) will yield roughly the same number of stitches and rows over a given measurement as a standard 'four-ply' yarn. This information is useful if you are substituting a yarn or designing a garment from scratch.

Finish

Fibres undergo a number of different finishes during the spinning process. They may be twisted loosely or firmly, for example, to produce a wide range of textures, from soft to very firm. In general, the tighter the twist, the harder-wearing the yarn.

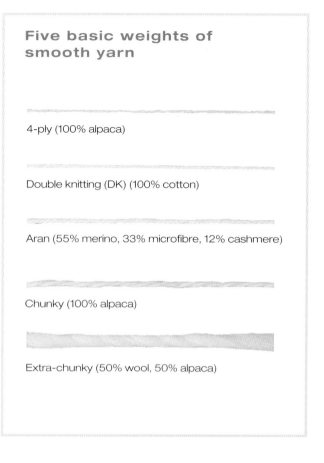

Five basic weights of smooth yarn

4-ply (100% alpaca)

Double knitting (DK) (100% cotton)

Aran (55% merino, 33% microfibre, 12% cashmere)

Chunky (100% alpaca)

Extra-chunky (50% wool, 50% alpaca)

Slubbed yarns are spun irregularly, so that they have thick and thin stretches. They add a pleasing variation of texture to plain stitch patterns, but are less successful than smooth yarns when worked in complex stitch patterns. This is because they tend to obscure the finer detail. Slubbed yarns can be quite effective in some larger lace and cable patterns, however.

Yarns are available in a variety of weights, plies and finishes.

**Understanding yarn
label symbols**

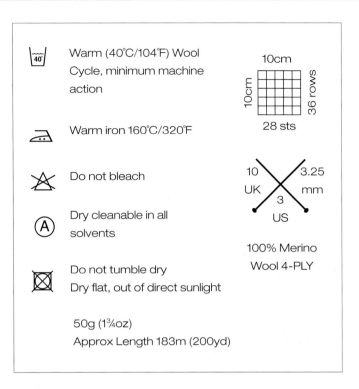

Symbol	Meaning
	Warm (40°C/104°F) Wool Cycle, minimum machine action
	Warm iron 160°C/320°F
	Do not bleach
	Dry cleanable in all solvents
	Do not tumble dry Dry flat, out of direct sunlight

10cm
10cm   36 rows
28 sts

10 UK   3.25 mm
3 US

100% Merino
Wool 4-PLY

50g (1¾oz)
Approx Length 183m (200yd)

This yarn label (right) gives all the information you need, including recommended needle size and suggested tension/gauge over stocking/stockinette stitch.

Bouclé yarns have a crinkly texture, which is produced by catching up one of the plies so that it forms a little loop around the other(s).

Knop yarns are similar in construction to boucle yarns, but are more irregular, with large loops at more widely spaced intervals. They produce a fuzzy, knobbly fabric.

Chenille yarns have a dense, velvety texture. Although very attractive, they are not easy to knit with.

Multicoloured effects can be produced by spinning together plies of different colours, or, for a subtler effect, different shades of the same colour. Flecked tweed yarns are the classic example of a multicoloured yarn. There is also a fashion for space-dyeing a yarn, so that the colour changes along its length. These are fun to use, although the results can be unpredictable.

Novelty yarns appear and disappear along with the latest trends. They may include woven ribbon and rag yarns, blends of metallic and cotton fibres, thin strands of suede – whatever is currently in vogue.

The choice of yarns available is dictated to some extent by fashion and it used to be the case that, when colour-patterned knitting became voguish, the more unusual textures, which do not lend themselves to such designs, were less commonly available. The internet has done much to remedy this, however, and it is now possible to source yarns of all types throughout the year and regardless of the latest trends.

Buying yarn

When buying yarn, it is very important to read the information on the yarn label. This information will include the fibre content, blocking/pressing instructions, recommendations on how to care for the garment, and the weight of the ball or skein. In some cases it may also give a recommended needle size and the number of stitches and rows produced in stocking/stockinette stitch using those needles (see Tension/gauge, page 25). This last information is very useful if you wish to substitute a different yarn for the one recommended by the pattern you are using.

One essential piece of information on the yarn label is the dye lot number. Make sure that all the yarn for any one garment is from the same lot – even a minor variation can be quite noticeable. Buy all the yarn you need at the same time, because the particular dye lot you are using may no longer be available later on if you should run out.

Equipment

You do not need a vast array of special equipment for hand knitting. The only essential items, of course, are the needles. These come in a variety of sizes (see page 189) and types, and you can build up a useful collection as you build on your skills. There are also a number of accessories that will come in handy occasionally.

Needles are made of several different materials: metal and plastic are the most common, but you can also find bamboo and wood alternatives. Metal needles are generally the easiest to work with, as the stitches slide along them easily; plastic tends to be rather sticky, although some people prefer them because they are warmer to the touch. You may find needles with rigid points that are attached to a flexible length of plastic. These are useful for knitting heavy items, as it means you do not have to support the whole weight of the garment yourself as you work.

Other types of needle include circular and double-pointed needles, for working in the round, and cable needles, used in cable-stitch patterns.

If you take good care of your needles they should last for many years. Store them in a large flat box or special needle case, so that they do not become bent. Never use a needle with a jagged point, as it can catch in the yarn, splitting the fibres.

Set of four double-pointed needles – used for tubular knitting and for medallions

Cable needle – the bend prevents the held stitches from slipping off

Circular needle (also called a twin pin) – used for tubular or straight knitting

Tape measure – used for checking that your worked pieces are of the correct tension/gauge.

Ring stitch markers – used to mark the beginning of rounds in tubular knitting and certain key points in a pattern

Stitch stoppers or needle guards – used to prevent the work from slipping off the needle when it is put away; an elastic band will serve the same purpose, but stoppers will also protect the needle points

Knitter's pins – used for holding two knitted sections together when seaming and for marking divisions on edges when picking up a specified number of stitches

Glass-headed pins – used for blocking knitting

Blunt-ended yarn needle – used for seams and for working embroidery on knitting

Bobbin – used for holding small amounts of yarn when working with two or more colours across a row

Stitch holder – a double-pointed needle or a length of yarn will also work; ordinary safety pins are best where only a few stitches need to be held

Needle gauge – useful for checking sizes of double-pointed and circular needles (marked only on the package) and when using needles sized according to a different system from the one used in the pattern

Other useful equipment includes scissors (a pair of embroidery scissors is also useful, especially when undoing work knitted with fuzzy yarns), a spray bottle for wet blocking, an iron, a cotton pressing cloth and an ironing board with a well-padded surface. A knitting bag is handy for keeping your knitting clean and tidy; some bags have wooden frames that allow them to stand on the floor when in use and fold up for carrying or storing. A folder for storing patterns is also useful.

Double-pointed needles are used to make socks in the round.

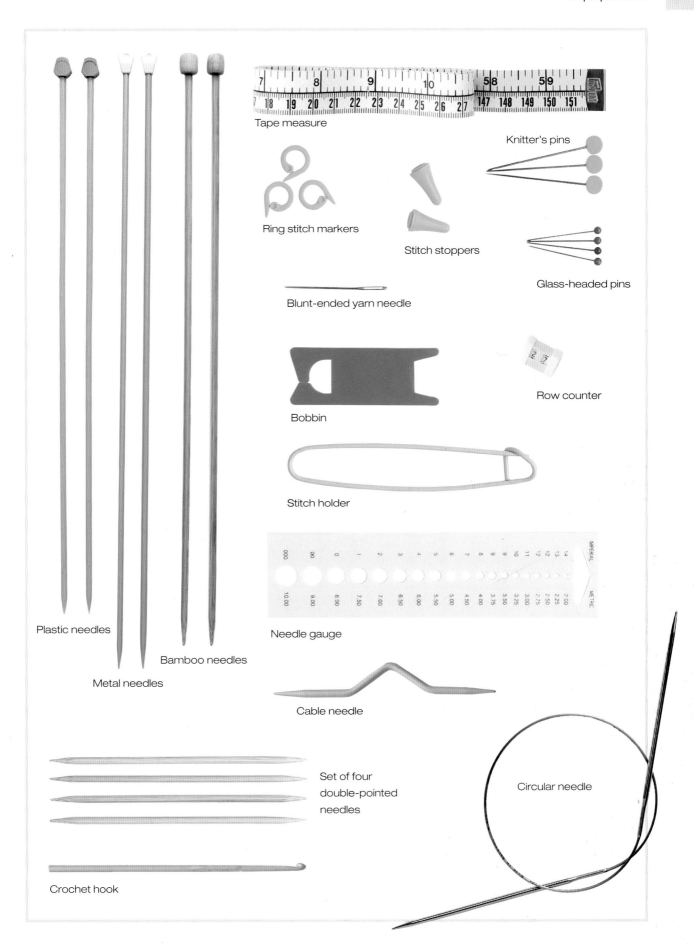

Tape measure

Knitter's pins

Ring stitch markers

Stitch stoppers

Glass-headed pins

Blunt-ended yarn needle

Bobbin

Row counter

Stitch holder

Plastic needles

Bamboo needles

Metal needles

Needle gauge

Cable needle

Set of four
double-pointed
needles

Circular needle

Crochet hook

Casting on

The first step when you start a piece of knitting is to place the required number of stitches on the needle. This is called 'casting on'. There are several different methods of casting on, the most common of which are the cable method and the thumb method. For both of these you need to hold the yarn as for knitting, so turn to page 18 to see which way of holding the yarn you prefer. The single cast-on is the simplest method; however, because the loops formed are difficult to work into evenly, it is not recommended for the novice. The double cast-on may look very complicated, but it has the benefit of needing no knitting experience. If you tend to cast on tightly, use needles a size or two larger than specified by the pattern for the casting on. Then change to the correct needles for the first row.

Slip knot

For the single, cable and thumb cast-ons, begin by making a slip knot on the needle. First make a loop in the yarn and draw one end of the yarn through with the point of the needle. Pull on both ends of the yarn to tighten the knot.

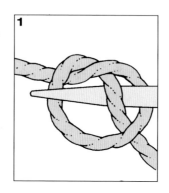

Single cast-on

This method produces a soft, flexible edge. Begin by making a slip knot near the end of the yarn. Wind the yarn around the thumb, and hold it with three fingers.

1 Bring the needle up through the loop as shown by the arrow.

2 Slip the thumb out of the loop, and use it to pull the yarn gently downwards, forming a stitch. Repeat steps 1 and 2.

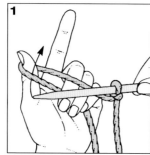

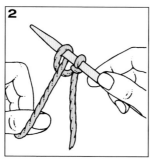

Cable method

This method produces an attractive, smooth edge, which is suitable for various fabrics. Begin with a slip knot near the end of the yarn.

1 Holding the loose end of the yarn firmly, insert the right-hand (RH) needle under the left, to the left of the slip knot. Take the main yarn under and over the (RH) needle, from left to right.

2 Draw the loop on the (RH) needle through to the front, and place it over the top of the left-hand (LH) needle.

3 Now insert the (RH) needle between the two stitches. Take the yarn under and over it, as in step 2, draw the loop through, and place it on the needle. Repeat step 3.

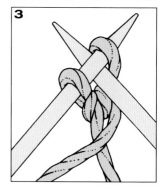

Thumb method

The edge produced by this method is the same as for the double cast-on. Multiply the number of stitches by 2cm (¾in) and measure off this length of yarn; make a slip knot slightly beyond this point. Hold the short end of yarn in your left hand as shown. Wrap the yarn from the ball around the little finger of your right hand, as for knitting (see page 18).

1 Take the point of the needle up under the front strand of yarn lying between the fingers and thumb of the left hand, following the direction of the arrow.

2 Now bring the right-hand (ball) yarn under and over the point of the needle. Holding both lengths fairly taut, bring the needle down through the left-hand loop as shown by the arrow.

3 Slip the thumb out of the loop, and use it to pull on the short end of yarn as shown to complete the new stitch. Repeat steps 1–3.

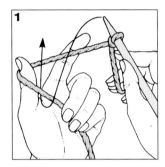
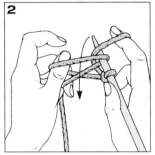
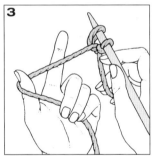

Double cast-on

Multiply the number of stitches required by 2cm (¾in), and measure off this length of yarn. Wind the yarn around the fingers of your left hand as shown: up between the third and little fingers, around the little finger, over all four fingers, then clockwise around the thumb; finally take the yarn between the second and third fingers and hold it gently but firmly. Spread the thumb and index finger apart to tension the yarn.

1 Slip the point of the needle up through the thumb loop.

2 Take it over and under the yarn extending to the index finger, thus forming a loop on the needle; as you do so, rotate your left hand towards you (you may do this instinctively, as it feels natural).

3 Bring the needle back through the thumb loop. Slip the thumb out of the loop and use it to pull down the free length of yarn. This completes the first stitch. Repeat steps 1–3. This produces a quite firm, yet flexible edge, which is good for ribbing.

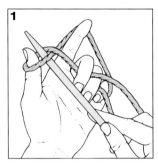

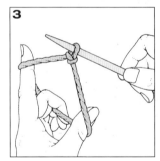

Holding the yarn

Once you have cast some stitches on to a needle, you are ready to begin knitting. There are several ways of holding the yarn and needles, and the two basic methods are shown here. The right-hand method of holding the yarn is used mainly in English-speaking countries, while the left-hand method is more commonly used in continental Europe. Each method produces the same results. Try both to see which you find more comfortable. It is a good idea to learn both methods, as for some multicoloured knitting patterns you need to work with two different colours at the same time. Whichever method you choose, wind the yarn loosely around the fingers to keep it slightly tensioned so that the stitches stay smooth and even. When starting out this may mean wrapping the yarn twice around your little finger.

Right-hand method

Take the needle with the cast-on stitches in the left hand. Wind the yarn around the fingers of the right hand as shown below.

Take the needle in the right hand so that it lies between the thumb and the rest of the hand as shown (in practice, the needle is often picked up before the yarn). Insert the needle into the first stitch on the LH needle, and slide the right hand forward to take the yarn around the point of the RH needle. In the photograph the needles are shown forming the knit stitch.

Left-hand method

Take the needle with the cast-on stitches in the right hand. Wind the yarn around the fingers of the left hand as shown.

Transfer the needle with the stitches to the left hand, and raise the index finger to tension the yarn. Take the working needle in the right hand, with the thumb in front and the fingers in back. Insert the needle into the first stitch, then rotate the left hand to bring the yarn around the point of the needle. In the photograph the needles are shown forming the knit stitch.

 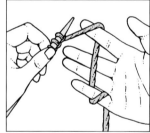  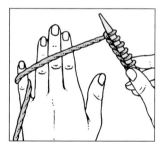

TIP

If you are left-handed, you may find the 'Continental' method of holding the yarn relatively easy to learn, as the work is more evenly divided between the two hands. The alternative is to use the right-hand method reversed, holding the needle with the stitches in the right hand, wrapping the yarn around the fingers of the left hand, and using the left hand to work the stitches. If you choose this method, you will find it helpful, when following the instructions in this book, to hold the book up to a mirror.

Knit and purl

Most knitting is based on combinations of just two basic stitches: the knit stitch and the purl stitch. Once you have mastered these two stitches, you can work many different stitch patterns. Begin by casting on about 25 or 30 stitches, using a double-knitting yarn in a light colour, preferably all wool or a wool mix, for its resilience. Practise the knit stitch until you can work it smoothly. Then practise the purl stitch.

The knit stitch

1 Hold the needle with the stitches to be knitted in the left hand with the yarn behind.

2 Insert the RH needle into a stitch from front to back. Take the yarn over it, forming a loop.

3 Now bring the needle and the new loop to the front of the work, and slide the original stitch off the LH needle.

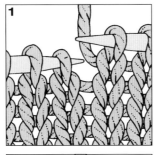

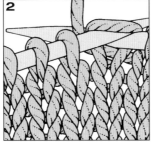

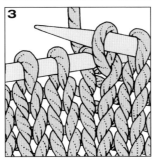

The purl stitch

1 Hold the stitches to be purled in the left hand, with the yarn at the front of the work.

2 Insert the RH needle through the front of the stitch, from back to front. Take the yarn over and under, forming a loop.

3 Take the needle and the new loop through to the back; and slide the original stitch off the LH needle.

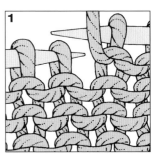

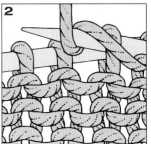

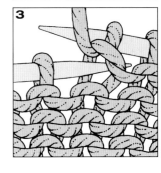

Garter stitch (right). This simple stitch pattern is produced by knitting every row. The fabric has a distinct horizontal ridge and is also quite stretchy.

Stocking/stockinette stitch (right). This is produced by knitting all the stitches on the right-side rows and purling on the wrong-side rows. The fabric is smooth and slightly elastic.

Stitch variations

Once you have mastered the knit and purl, it is easy to learn a few variations on these basic techniques. One of these is working into the back of the stitch rather than into the front of it. You may use this technique when increasing stitches (see pages 28–30) and in some stitch patterns. It is possible to produce a variation of stocking/stockinette stitch by working all the knit stitches through the back; you work the purl stitches through the front as usual. The resulting fabric is unusually firm. Another technique is simply to slip a stitch off the left-hand needle on to the right without working it. Slipped stitches are used in some methods of decreasing and in some multicolour patterns (see page 61).

Knitting through the back of the loop

Insert the RH needle behind the LH needle and through the back of the stitch, and take the yarn under and over the needle, forming a knit stitch in the usual way. Pull the new stitch through, and slip the original stitch off the LH needle. The new stitch is slightly twisted.

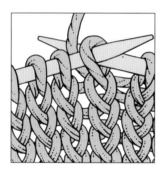

Slipping a stitch knitwise

Insert the needle into the front of the stitch as if to knit it, but do not form a new stitch; simply slip the original stitch on to the RH needle. The same technique is used to slip a purl stitch knitwise. Unless the pattern instructions state otherwise, the yarn is held as for the preceding stitch: at the back if this was a knit stitch; at the front if it was a purl stitch.

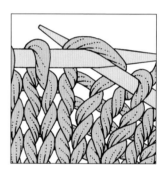

Purling through the back of the loop

Turn the RH needle briefly to point from left to right, then insert it from back to front through the back of the loop as shown. Form a purl stitch in the usual way, and slip the original stitch off the LH needle. The new stitch is slightly twisted.

Slipping a stitch purlwise

Insert the needle into the stitch from back to front, as if you were going to purl it, then simply slip it on to the RH needle. The same technique is used to slip a purl stitch purlwise. Unless the pattern states otherwise, the yarn is held as for the preceding stitch.

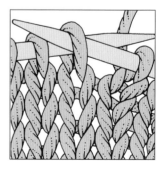

Casting/binding off

To end a piece of knitting, you 'cast/bind off' the stitches. This technique is also used to reduce the number of stitches at the side of a piece of knitting – for example, when shaping an armhole – or in the middle, when working a horizontal buttonhole. There are several methods of casting/binding off, but the one shown here is most common. This basic method alters slightly when casting/binding off a ribbed fabric, where it produces a softer, more elastic edge than the basic method. To avoid casting/binding off too tightly, and producing an edge that is narrower than the width of the fabric, use a needle one or two sizes larger than those used for the main fabric. When you have learned the basic cast-/bind-off method, try the advanced methods on pages 82–83.

Basic cast-/bind-off

1 Knit the first two stitches. Slip the LH needle into the first stitch on the RH needle.

2 Lift the first stitch over the second stitch and off the needle. Repeat steps 1 and 2 until one stitch remains. Break the yarn and draw it firmly through the last stitch.

If casting/binding off on the purled side (the wrong side) of a stocking/stockinette stitch fabric, you may prefer to purl the stitches instead of knitting them. Here, the loops of the cast-/bound-off edge will lie toward the knit side of the work.

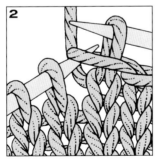

Casting/binding off in rib

Work all the stitches as if continuing in the pattern: so purl stitches will be purled, rather than knitted. Lift the first stitch over the second as usual.

Achieving an even cast-/bind-off in rib is not easy, even for experienced knitters. Practise on a spare piece of ribbing, keeping a fairly loose tension/gauge and working evenly.

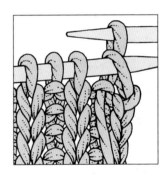

You might feel that you can knit and purl, but are not confident enough to follow a knitting pattern. It is true that patterns often look very complex and may even appear to be written in a foreign language. However, it is relatively easy to learn this language, as you are about to discover. All but the simplest projects contain increases, decreases and seams, and many need you to be able to pick up stitches or make a buttonhole. All of these techniques are described on the following pages. And, most important for a beginner, there are instructions on correcting any mistakes you happen to make.

Following a pattern

Selecting a pattern

First of all, it is important to select a pattern that is appropriate for your level of ability so that it will be successful and encourage you to develop your knitting skills. If you are choosing your first pattern, try to select something that is not absolutely dependent on perfect sizing and shaping. Also, do not choose a very complicated stitch pattern.

Size

Check that the sizes given with a pattern include one that is suitable for your measurements. This will allow some room for movement when wearing the garment, known as 'ease' or 'tolerance'. If several sets of figures are given, the smallest size is always indicated first, with larger ones in brackets. It is a good idea to circle each figure that refers to your size.

Materials and equipment

A printed pattern will specify all the materials and equipment necessary to complete the garment. It will state the amount and type of yarn, needle sizes, the correct tension/gauge (see page 25), and any extras required, such as buttons or zips. While still learning to knit, it is wise to choose the exact yarn specified in the pattern. Later, when you are more experienced, you can often substitute a different yarn for the one specified. For guidance on buying yarn, see pages 10–13.

Sequence of working

The pattern will indicate the order in which you should work the pieces. Always stick to this order. Often some instructions in one piece relate to those already completed. You should also sew the pieces together in the order suggested, because this may relate to some further work such as a neckband or collar.

Get into the habit of checking your work as you go along, especially if it has a complicated stitch pattern. Lay it out flat in good light and look at it carefully. By checking the number of stitches on the needle you can quickly tell whether everything is going according to plan or not.

Knitting language

All knitting patterns use abbreviations and symbols of various kinds in order to save space. These are fairly standard, although you will find some differences in patterns produced in different English-speaking countries and in different spinners' patterns and knitting books. A full list of the abbreviations used in this book is given on page 6. Special abbreviations are explained at the beginning of a pattern.

In addition to abbreviations, patterns use symbols such as ( ), [ ], and * *. These may contain variations for different garment sizes, or they may enclose a set of instructions that are to be repeated. For example, '*K1, P1, rep from * to end.'

Sections of a pattern that are to be repeated may use two or more asterisks, to indicate repeats within repeats. Although this all sounds very confusing to the beginner, you will find as you gain experience that such symbols are very easy to understand.

Knitting a simple shape, such as a blanket, can provide a good opportunity to experiment with colour and texture.

Tension/gauge

A most important part of any knitting pattern is where it states the necessary 'tension/gauge'. This is the number of stitches and rows, over a given measurement, obtained by the designer of that pattern. It will be given in a form such as: '21 sts and 30 rows to 10cm (4in), measured over st st on 4mm needles'. Sometimes the tension/gauge is measured 'over pattern' – that is, over the stitch pattern used for the main part of the garment. It is essential to check your tension/gauge in order for the garment to come out the correct size. The best way to do this, is to knit a swatch before beginning the garment itself.

Knitting a swatch

Cast on a few more stitches than stated by the pattern for the tension/gauge. Work in the specified pattern stitch, using the specified needles, until the work measures just over 10cm (4in), then cast/bind off.

Pin the swatch to a flat, padded surface, without stretching it. For highly textured or lacy patterns, it may be necessary to block the work (see page 35) to make it as smooth as the finished garment will be.

Insert a pin a few stitches in from one edge. Count off the number of stitches required for the tension/gauge and insert another pin. Measure the distance between the pins. It should be 10cm (4in) or the measurement given. If the measurement is greater, your tension/gauge is too loose, and you should change to smaller needles. If it is shorter, your tension/gauge is too tight, and you should change to larger needles.

Measure the row tension/gauge in the same way, although if it is given over stocking/stockinette stitch, you may find it easier to count it on the purl side of the work. The row tension/gauge is usually less important than the stitch tension/gauge, because shaping instructions are normally given after a certain measurement has been achieved, and not after a given number of rows. However, some patterns require a given number of pattern repeats to be completed at certain shaping points, and in such cases if the row tension/gauge varies from that required, the proportions of the garment will be incorrect.

It is a good idea to re-check your tension/gauge during the course of knitting a garment, which you can do on a completed section.

Complex stitch patterns

To make a swatch for a complex stitch pattern, look at the first row that contains a repeated group of stitches and calculate how many stitches are in the repeat. For example: '*(K1, P1, K1) into first st, P3tog, rep from * to end.' When you have followed the first instruction, in brackets, you will have 3 stitches; from the second, 'purl 3 together', you will have 1 stitch. Add the 1 to the 3 to get the number of stitches in one repeat: 4.

The number of stitches to cast on must be divisible by 4 and include a few stitches more than those specified for the tension/gauge. Add any edge stitches given in the pattern; these will be found outside the asterisks. Cast on this number and work as instructed until the swatch measures just over 10cm (4in).

If the stitches are hard to count, tie loops of yarn at the beginning and end of the specified number of stitches and rows. Then measure the tension/gauge between these markers.

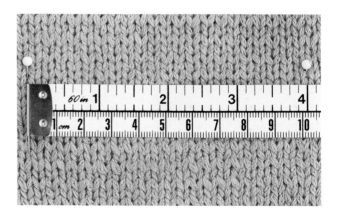

Measuring the distance between a given number of stitches on a knitted swatch will indicate if your tension is too loose or too tight.

Correcting mistakes

It is a good idea to learn how to deal effectively with mistakes. Keep a crochet hook within easy reach, as you can use it to pick up dropped stitches. A cable needle is also useful for holding a loose stitch while you deal with a problem. After correcting a mistake, always count the stitches to make sure that you have the right number.

Picking up in knit

If the work is in stocking/stockinette stitch, insert the crochet hook from front to back through the lowest stitch in the ladder, pick up the strand as shown, and pull it through to make a new stitch; repeat to the top of the ladder, and place the last stitch on the LH needle, making sure it is turned the correct way.

Unpicking stitches

If you find a mistake a few rows down, it is feasible to unpick the work stitch by stitch until you reach the mistake, then correct it and proceed as usual.

1 To unpick a knit stitch, put the LH needle through the stitch below. Pull the RH needle out of the stitch above it, and pull the yarn out of the loop.

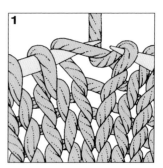

2 To unpick a purl stitch, the process is essentially the same as for a knit stitch, but you hold the yarn in front of the work.

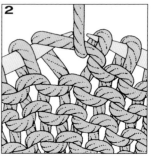

Picking up in purl

In some patterns you will need to pick up purl stitches when retrieving a ladder. The technique is basically the same as for a knit stitch, but you insert the hook from back to front as shown.

Unravelling

For a mistake more than a few rows down, unravel the work to one or two rows below the mistake, ending with the yarn at the RH edge. In some patterns it is easier to work from the right side of the fabric; in others, including stocking/stockinette stitch, it is easier to work on the wrong side, as shown.

Insert the needle into the stitch below the RH loop from back to front, and pull out the loop. Continue in this way to the end of the row.

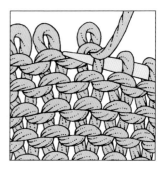

When picking up stitches after unravelling, use a needle two or three sizes smaller than those used for the knitting to avoid pulling the stitches out of shape.

Selvedges

A selvedge is a specially worked edge on a piece of knitting. You may add one to give a smooth, firm edge on a fabric, such as stocking/stockinette stitch, which would otherwise have a rather loose one, and so make the edges easier to handle when sewing seams. Or you might use a selvedge to give a decorative finish to a piece of knitting that is not going to have a seam – a scarf, for example. This will also prevent the edges from curling.

Single chain edge

This selvedge gives a smooth edge and is appropriate for pieces that will be joined edge to edge (see page 36) or where stitches will be picked up (see page 33).

For the right side: slip the first stitch knitwise; knit the last stitch.

For the wrong side: slip the first stitch purlwise; purl the last stitch.

Single garter edge

This method produces a firm edge on fabrics that tend to be loose, and is especially well suited to backstitch seams (see page 36).

For the right and wrong sides: knit the first and the last stitch.

Double garter edge

This is a decorative edge that lies flat. Allow 2 extra stitches for each edge.

For the right and wrong sides: slip the first stitch knitwise and knit the second stitch. At the end of the row, knit the last 2 stitches.

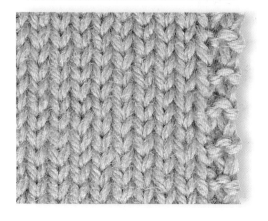

Increases and decreases

There are many different methods of increasing and decreasing, and they are used for various purposes. You might use a series of increases or decreases at the edge of a piece of knitting or across a row to shape it. You might also use them decoratively to produce many interesting stitch patterns. When used for stitch patterns, increases and decreases are normally paired, so that the number of stitches on the needle remains the same.

Increasing

The three increases shown on pages 28–29 are discreet and inconspicuous. The increases on page 30 are 'decorative increases', which make a hole in the fabric and are used mainly in lace patterns. They are produced by taking the yarn over or around the needle, depending on the starting position of the yarn.

Bar increase – knitwise

(abbreviated inc 1)

A bar increase involves working twice into the same stitch. Whether worked on a knit row or a purl row, this produces a tiny horizontal strand on the knit side of the work. If worked a few stitches in from the edge, it can have a decorative effect.

1 Knit into the front of the stitch as usual, but do not slip the stitch off the needle at this point. Instead, knit again into the same stitch through the back of the loop.

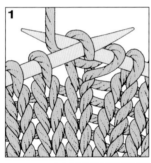

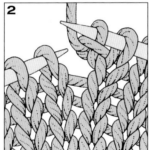

2 Slip the original stitch off the LH needle. Two stitches have been made from one. This method of increasing is often used to create fullness above the ribbing – known as a 'mass increase'.

Bar increase – purlwise

(abbreviated inc 1)

1 Purl the stitch in the usual way, but do not slip the stitch off the needle.

2 Purl again into the same stitch through the back of the loop – twisting the stitch as shown here.

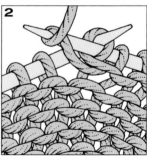

3 Slip the original stitch off the LH needle. In either a knit or purl bar increase the little bar produced on the knit side will appear to the right of the first of the two stitches. Therefore, if you 'inc 1' into the 4th stitch from the RH edge, you should work across the row until there are 5 stitches remaining, and work the inc 1 into the first of these 5 stitches. On the knit side the bar will appear 4 stitches in from each edge.

Making one knit stitch
(abbreviated M1)

1 Insert the LH needle from front to back under the strand lying between the two adjacent stitches on the LH and RH needles.

2 Knit into the back of the new loop just formed on the LH needle.

3 Now slip the picked-up loop off the needle.

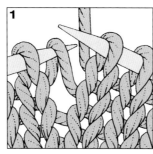

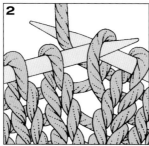

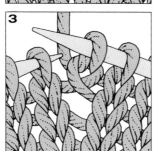

Making one purl stitch
(abbreviated M1)

1 Insert the LH needle from front to back under the strand lying between the two adjacent stitches on the LH and RH needles.

2 Purl into the back of the new loop just formed, twisting it as shown to make this possible.

3 Now slip the picked-up loop off the LH needle.

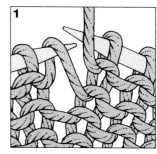

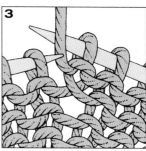

Lifted increase – knitwise

Like the 'M1' increase, this type of increase is inconspicuous.

1 With the RH needle, pull up the stitch lying directly below the next stitch on the LH needle, from front to back, and knit into it.

2 Now knit into the next stitch on the LH needle.

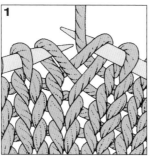

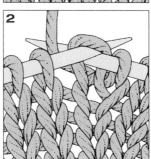

Lifted increase – purlwise

1 With the RH needle, pull up the stitch lying directly below the next stitch on the LH, from back to front, and purl into it.

2 Now purl into the next stitch on the LH needle.

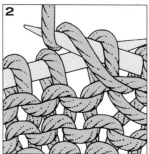

Yarn forward
(abbreviated yf)

This is worked between two knit stitches.

1 Bring the yarn to the front of the work, then back over the RH needle.

2 Now knit the next stitch in the usual way – this will form an extra loop on the needle.

3 On the next row, purl into this loop as if it were a stitch (or work as instructed in the pattern).

Yarn over needle
(abbreviated yon)

This is worked between a purl stitch and a knit stitch; the yarn will be at the front of the work. Take the yarn back over the RH needle. Knit the next stitch in the usual way. On the next row, work into the new loop as instructed by the pattern.

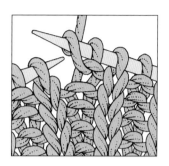

Yarn round needle
(abbreviated yrn)

This is worked between two purl stitches, or between a knit and a purl stitch. Begin with the yarn at the front of the work.

1 Take the yarn over the RH needle and to the front, taking it completely around the needle.

2 Purl the next stitch as usual – this will form an extra loop on the needle.

3 On the next row work into this loop as if it were a stitch.

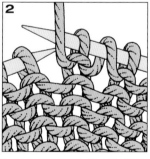

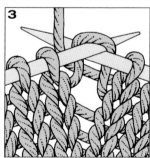

The yarn forward increase is used in creating eyelets, as in this quatrefoil eyelet pattern (see page 173).

Decreasing

There are fewer methods of decreasing than of increasing. Like increases, however, each method of decreasing produces a different effect on a fabric and can be used either inconspicuously to help shape the overall piece, or decoratively.

On raglan armholes a decorative type of decreasing – called 'fully fashioned' shaping – is popular. Here, you work the decreases two stitches in from the edge. At the right-hand edge you work a slipstitch decrease on the third and fourth stitches from the edge; at the left-hand edge you knit the third and fourth stitches together.

Knitting two stitches together
(abbreviated K2tog)

1 First, insert the RH needle knitwise into the second stitch on the LH needle and then into the first stitch.

2 Now knit the 2 stitches together, and then slip the original stitch off the LH needle.

Purling two stitches together
(abbreviated P2tog)

1 First, insert the RH needle purlwise into the first stitch on the LH needle and then into the second stitch.

2 Now purl the 2 stitches together, and then slip the original stitch off the LH needle.

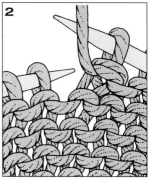

Knitting together through back loops
(abbreviated K2tog tbl)

When stitches are knitted together normally, they slant to the right. For patterns that require a slant to the left, insert the RH needle through the backs of the first and second stitches on the LH needle. Knit the stitches together.

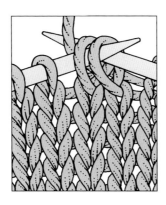

Purling together through back loops
(abbreviated P2tog tbl)

When stitches are purled together normally, they slant to the right on the knit side of the work. To achieve a slant to the left, insert the RH needle from the back to the front through the second stitch and then the first stitch. Now purl the two stitches together.

Slipped stitch decrease – knit

Like knitting two together tbl, this produces a distinct slant to the left. Instructions are: 'slip one, knit one, pass slipped stitch over', or 'sl 1, K1, psso' (alternatively 'skpo' or 'skp').

1 Slip the first stitch on the LH needle knitwise.

2 Knit the next stitch.

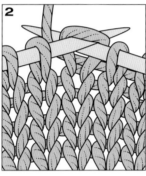

3 Now insert the LH needle into the slipped stitch, and lift it over the knitted stitch and off the RH needle.

Slipped stitch decrease – purl

The instructions are: 'slip one, purl one, pass slipped stitch over', or 'sl 1, P1, psso'.

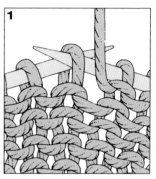

1 With the yarn at the front of your work, slip the first stitch purlwise.

2 Purl the next stitch in the usual way.

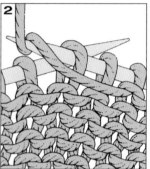

3 Now insert the LH needle into the slipped stitch and lift it over the purled stitch and off the RH needle to finish.

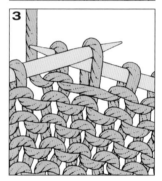

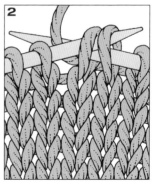

Slip, slip, knit decrease
(abbreviated ssk)

Similar to an ordinary knitwise slipped stitch decrease, this produces a smoother effect, which may be preferred in some lace patterns.

1 Slip the first stitch knitwise, then slip the second knitwise.

2 Insert LH needle into the front of the two slipped stitches, without removing them from the RH; knit them together through the backs of the loops with the RH needle.

Picking up stitches

You can hold stitches on a spare needle or stitch holder and work into them later, once another part of the garment is complete. Using a double-pointed needle allows you to work into the stitches from either end. Your pattern will specify how many stitches to pick up, and it is important to space them evenly.

Picking up stitches on a cast-/bound-off edge

(abbreviated K up)

1 Secure the yarn just under the RH edge. Insert the needle from front to back through the first edge stitch.

2 Take the yarn under and over the needle to form a loop, and draw the loop through to the front. Repeat to the end. The first row will be worked on the wrong side.

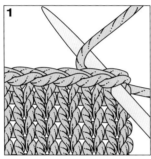

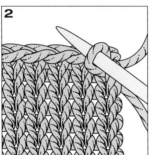

Picking up stitches along a side (row-end) edge

For this method, you will probably need to plan the spacing of the stitches as for a curved edge (see below), since working into every stitch or every other stitch may yield too many or too few. Work one stitch in from the edge without encroaching on the next line of stitches.

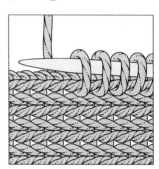

Picking up stitches with a crochet hook

Secure the yarn just under the LH edge. Using a crochet hook, pull a loop through to the front of the work. Insert the needle into this loop, and pull the yarn slightly to make it snug. Repeat all along the edge.

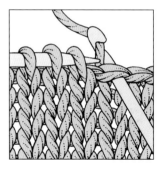

Left-handed knitters

Left-handed knitters may prefer to work this method from the wrong side of the work, moving from right to left.

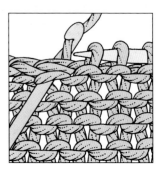

To pick up stitches on a curved edge, use large pins to mark the halfway point of the edge, then divide each of these two sections in half. Divide the number of stitches to be picked up by the number of sections, and space these groups of stitches accordingly.

Buttonholes

Making buttonholes is an important skill to learn and is not difficult. There are three main types: the eyelet buttonhole, used on baby clothes; the horizontal buttonhole, often worked in a ribbed band on the front edge of a cardigan; and the vertical buttonhole, which is best used decoratively, as it is the weakest of the three types.

Horizontal buttonhole

1 Work to the position for the buttonhole and cast/bind off the specified number of stitches. Work to the end.

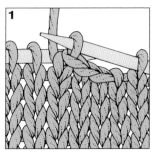

2 On the wrong side, cast on the same number of stitches as were cast/bound off, using the single cast-on method (see page 16).

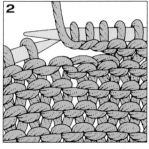

3 On the next row, work into the back of the cast-on stitches for a neat finished effect.

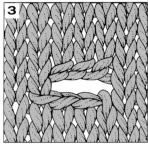

Vertical buttonhole

1 Work up to the position of the buttonhole, and slip the remaining stitches on to a stitch holder. Turn the work and continue for the specified number of rows, ending with a right-side row. Do not break off the yarn.

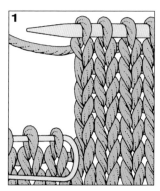

2 Join a length of yarn to the buttonhole edge of the held stitches. Using the needle in the RH stitches, work to the end, then turn and continue until there is one row less than on the RH side.

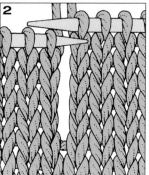

3 Fasten off the second length of yarn, and continue to the end of the row.

Eyelet buttonhole

1 Work to the position of the buttonhole. Bring the yarn forward (see page 30) to make a new stitch. Insert the needle knitwise into the next 2 stitches.

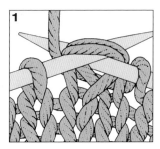

2 Knit the stitches together to decrease one stitch and work into the new loop on the next row.

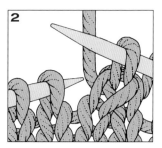

Blocking and pressing

Having spent hours knitting a garment, it is important not to skimp on the finishing process. Take care at this stage to ensure that your knitting is shown to its best advantage and that your final garment is one you can be proud of.

Equipment

Before joining pieces of knitting, you need to block them to shape, and possibly press them. Pattern instructions usually specify how to treat the various pieces. For blocking or pressing you need a firm, flat surface padded with a blanket and a sheet or towel – you can use an ironing board for small pieces. You also need rustproof pins.

Wet blocking

Pin the piece to your flat surface, right side up and following the measurements given in the pattern. Make sure that the knitting runs straight and that the shape is not distorted. Insert pins at intervals of 2cm (⅜in), at an angle through the edge stitch of the knitting into the padding. Do not pin the ribbing.

Dampen the work thoroughly with cool water, using a spray bottle. Leave the knitting to dry completely.

Steam blocking

This treatment is suitable for natural fibres. First pin the pieces to your work surface as for wet blocking. To apply steam, use either a steam iron and a dry cloth or a dry iron and a damp cloth. Place the cloth over the work and hold the iron just above it, allowing the steam to penetrate the knitting. Allow the work to dry before removing the pins.

Pressing

Pin the pieces wrong side up to your flat surface, using pins with ordinary heads. Do not pin the ribbing. Place the pins close together and insert them diagonally into the padded surface.

Use a steam iron and a dry cloth. For natural-synthetic blends use a dry, cool iron over a dry cloth. Do not slide the iron over the surface; instead, place it lightly on one area for a second, then lift it off. Allow the work to cool before taking it off the surface.

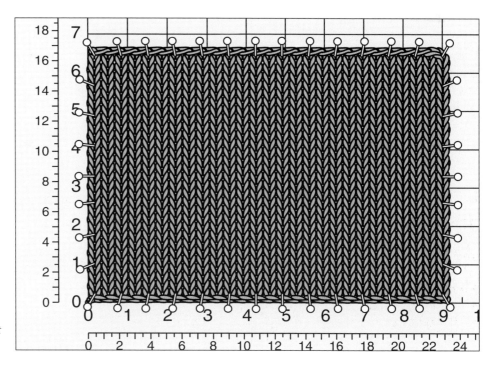

Pin the piece carefully so that the knitting runs straight.

Seams

There are several different ways of sewing pieces of knitting together, each suitable for different parts of a garment. An edge-to-edge seam, for example, is ideal for joining a buttonhole band to a front edge as there is little bulk and the seam is almost invisible. Backstitch is the preferred method where strength is required – as in a side seam. You might graft some edges rather than sewing them together; for this advanced technique see page 84. You can sew a garment with the same yarn as you used for the knitting. However, if this yarn is a chunky weight, you should opt for a lighter-weight yarn. Always secure the yarn with a couple of overcast stitches.

Edge-to-edge seam

This seam stitch is also known as mattress stitch.

Place both pieces right side up on a flat surface.

1 Secure the yarn to the wrong side, on the RH edge, and bring it through to the right side between the edge stitch and the next stitch on the first row of knitting.

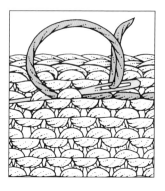

2 Take the yarn across and under the stitch loop between the edge stitch and the next stitch on the first row on the LH edge; draw the edges together, then work between the edge stitch and the next stitch on the second row on the RH edge. Now continue along the seam, pulling the yarn gently to bring the two edges together smoothly.

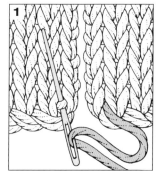

Backstitch seam

Pin the two pieces together with right sides facing.

Secure the yarn to the RH corner.

Work from right to left, taking the yarn across two stitches on the under side, then back over one stitch on top, so that the stitches meet end to end as shown. On the other side, the stitches overlap.

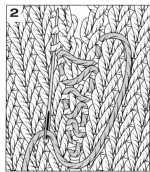

These mittens (see pages 120–123) can be finished using either a backstitch or an edge-to-edge seam.

Setting in a sleeve

You set a sleeve with a curved sleeve head into the armhole after joining adjacent seams.

1 Turn the main part of the garment wrong side out. Insert a pin into the front and back edges halfway between the two seams. Turn the sleeve right side out, and insert pins at the centre point and halfway down.

2 Position the sleeve inside the armhole, and pin the edges together, matching the pins and seams. Add more pins around the edge, placing them about 2–3cm (¾–1in) apart and easing the sleeve to fit the armhole, if necessary. You may wish to tack/baste the edges together.

3 Work around the armhole, about 5mm (¼in) from the edge, in backstitch and working from the sleeve side.

Alternative method: If you prefer, join just the shoulder seam, then sew in the sleeve head, then join the remaining seams.

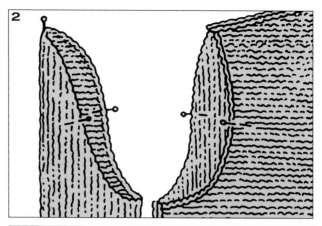

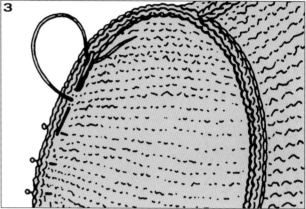

Darning in ends

You should darn ends left from knitting or seams into the work, usually along the edge. Use a blunt-ended yarn needle, to avoid splitting the stitches. Work a small stitch in the edge, then take the yarn through the edge stitches for a short distance and cut it off. For extra security, take it back in the opposite direction. If the yarn is too thick for the needle eye or too short to manipulate, use a crochet hook to pull it through the stitches.

Darning in ends in a motif

In intarsia knitting (see page 62), when you complete a motif, you are left with two lengths of yarn: one from the motif and one from the background. (The remaining background colour is used to continue the knitting.) Cut these two ends, leaving enough for the darning (it need not go all the way around a motif unless the difference in thickness would be visible on the right side). Weave the ends through the edge of the motif, making sure that the darker yarn does not show through the lighter knitting.

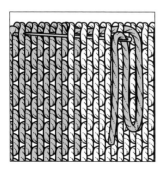

Once you have mastered the basic knitting skills and can follow a pattern, you are ready to move on to more adventurous stitch patterns. The techniques described here are quite demanding, but the results are worth the effort. With a little practice you can produce gracefully coiling cables, large and small bobbles, knitted smocking and shaggy looped pile fabrics. It is worth experimenting with different yarns to see how many varied effects are possible using these stitches. For example, cables are often worked in Aran yarn, as part of a traditional Aran-style sweater; but they can look beautiful in a glossy cotton or silk yarn, and also lend themselves well to mohair and angora yarns.

Special textures

Twisted stitches and cables

Some of the most beautiful stitch patterns involve crossing stitches over each other. You can cross stitches in many different ways. For example, you can work some crossing techniques entirely on the main pair of needles, where the technique is referred to as 'twisting' the stitches. You can twist up to four stitches to produce mock cables that are virtually indistinguishable from those produced with a cable needle. It is important, when twisting stitches, to keep a loose tension on the yarn on the twist row and on those preceding and following it. This makes the work easier and reduces strain on the yarn. When cabling, always use a cable needle no larger than the main needles, to avoid distorting the stitches. Cables may coil to the right, called 'cable back', or to the left, called 'cable forward'. You can work the basic cable over 4, 6 or 8 stitches.

Twisted stitches and a cable are shown in this sample. On the left, two stitches have been twisted right on every fourth row. On the right, a 'cable 4 forward' has been worked on every sixth row.

Achieving cable effects

You can achieve different effects by varying the number of rows between cable rows, although you use the same technique whatever the number. Working the cable every sixth row produces a graceful coil; on every fourth row, a thick, rope-like effect; on every tenth or twelfth row, a flat effect like a twisted ribbon. You can produce a novel effect by using a contrasting colour for half of the cable stitches.

Variations on cabling

You can use the basic cable technique to move a single stitch or a group of stitches across the fabric, forming more complex cable and lattice patterns. The illustrations on page 42 show how to move a single knit stitch to the right or the left on a background of reverse stocking/stockinette stitch. You can use the same basic method to move different numbers of stitches at a time. To become familiar with cabling techniques, make a sample using Aran or double-knitting yarn.

Twist 2 right
(abbreviated Tw2R)

1 Take the RH needle in front of the first stitch on the LH needle and knit into the second stitch. Do not let the first stitch slip off the needle.

2 Now knit into the first stitch and slip both stitches off the LH needle. On the next row, purl into the twisted stitches as usual. The stitches twist to the right.

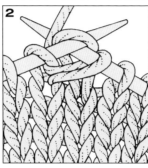

Twist 2 right purlwise
(abbreviated Tw2PR)

1 Take the RH needle in front of the first stitch on the LH needle and purl into the second stitch.

2 Purl into the first stitch, then slip both stitches off the LH needle. On the next row, knit into the twisted stitches as usual. The stitches will twist to the right on the knit side of the work.

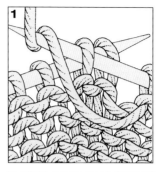

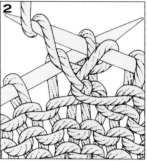

Twist 2 left
(abbreviated Tw2L)

1 Take the RH needle behind the first stitch on the LH needle, and knit into the second stitch, working through the back of the loop.

2 Knit into the first stitch, also through the back of the loop. On the next row, purl into the twisted stitches as usual. The stitches will now twist to the left.

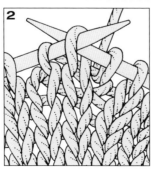

Twist 2 left purlwise
(abbreviated Tw2PL)

1 Take the RH needle and yarn behind the first stitch on the LH needle, and purl into the back of the second stitch, twisting it as shown. Take care not to let the first stitch slip off the needle.

2 Purl into the front of the first stitch, and slip both stitches off the needle. On the next row, knit into the twisted stitches as usual. The stitches twist to the left on the knit side of the work.

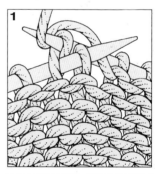

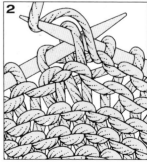

Mock cable back

This mock cable contains 4 stitches.

1 Take the RH needle in front of the first 2 stitches and knit the third stitch. Knit the fourth stitch. Leave all 4 stitches on the LH needle. Knit the second stitch on the LH needle.

2 Now knit the first stitch and slip all 4 stitches off the needle. On the following row, purl these stitches, remembering to keep the yarn tension fairly loose. The resulting cable will twist to the right.

Mock cable forward

For this mock cable, knit the third and fourth stitches through the back of the loops. Then knit the first stitch through the front in the usual way, slip it off the needle, knit the second stitch through the front and slip all stitches off the needle. The resulting cable twists to the left.

Cross 2 back

(abbreviated Cr2B)

1 Slip the purl stitch immediately before the knit stitch on to a cable needle and hold it at the back of the work. Knit the knit stitch.

2 Purl the stitch from the cable needle.

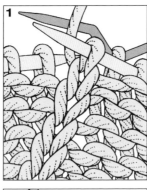

Cross 2 forward

(abbreviated Cr2F)

1 Slip the knit stitch on to the cable needle and hold it at the front of the work. Purl the purl stitch.

2 Knit the stitch from the cable needle.

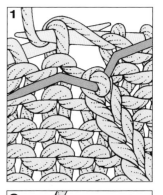

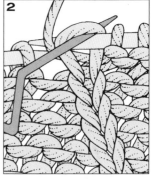

Cable 6 back
(abbreviated C6B)

1 Work to the position of the cable, slip the next 3 stitches on to the cable needle and hold them at the back of the work. Knit the next 3 stitches.

2 Knit the 3 stitches from the cable needle. On the next row, purl these stitches as usual. The cable coils to the right.

Cable 6 forward
(abbreviated C6F)

1 Work to the position of the cable, slip the next 3 stitches on to the cable needle and hold them at the front of the work. Knit the next 3 stitches.

2 Knit the 3 stitches from the cable needle. On the next row, purl these stitches as usual. The cable coils to the left.

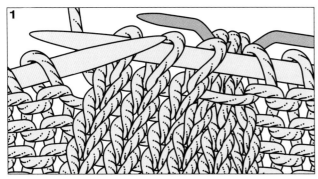
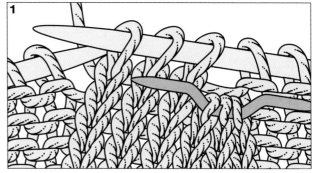

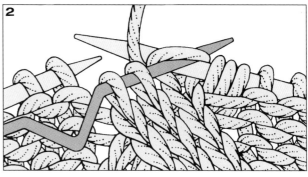

The pullover on pages 128–131 features a prominent single cable, ideal for a beginner.

Bobbles and knots

Different sizes and shapes of bobble can be made by making several stitches out of one stitch and then decreasing back to a single stitch, after working one or more rows on the increased stitches. You usually work the extra rows on the bobble alone, which makes the bobble stand out from the background, as it is attached only at the top and bottom. For a softer bobble, work the increased stitches along with the background fabric. Small bobbles or knots are made by decreasing the increased stitches.

Bobble – method 1

This bobble is worked in reverse stocking/stockinette stitch and is shown on a stocking/stockinette stitch fabric. For a stocking/stockinette stitch bobble, reverse the 'knit' and 'purl' instructions in steps 2 and 3.

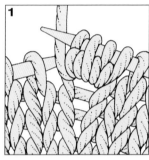

1 Knit, purl, knit and purl into the same stitch, thus making 4 stitches out of one. Turn the work.

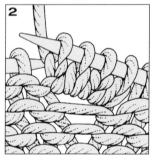

2 Knit these 4 stitches. Turn. Purl the stitches. Turn again.

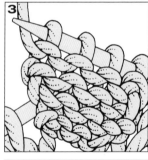

3 Repeat step 2 once more. The right (purl) side of the bobble is now facing.

4 With the LH needle, lift the second, third and fourth stitches over the first, thus decreasing back to one stitch and completing the bobble.

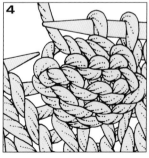

Bobble – method 2

This bobble is slightly flatter than that shown in Method 1.

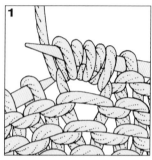

1 Knit 1, yarn forward, knit 1, yarn forward, knit 1. Turn. Purl the stitches. Turn again.

2 Knit the stitches. Turn. Purl 2 together, purl 1, purl 2 together: 3 stitches. Turn.

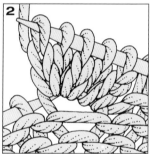

3 Slip 1, knit 2 together, then pass the slipped stitch over.

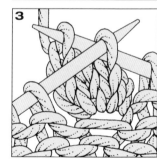

Knot – method 1

This small bobble, or knot, is produced in essentially the same way as the Method 1 bobble opposite, but the increased stitches are immediately decreased.

1 Knit, purl, knit, purl and knit into the stitch, thus making a total of 5 stitches out of one.

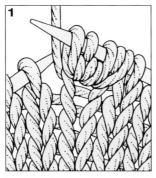

2 With the LH needle, lift the second, third, fourth and fifth stitches over the first one, thus decreasing back to one stitch and completing the knot.

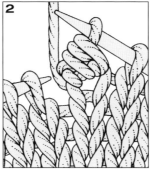

Knot – method 2

This method produces a slightly flatter and smoother knot than Method 1, above.

1 Knit into the front, back, front and back of the stitch, thus making 4 stitches out of one. With the LH needle, lift the second stitch over the first one.

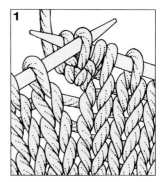

2 Lift the third and fourth stitches over the first one, completing the knot.

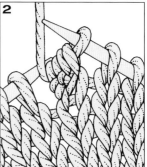

Contrasting bobbles and knots

To work a bobble or knot in a contrasting colour, simply tie the new colour to the first colour at the position for the bobble on the wrong side of the work, drop the first colour and work the bobble in the new colour. When the bobble is completed, break off the yarn and tie the ends together securely. When the knitting is completed, darn the ends into the wrong side. If working a series of bobbles across a row at short intervals, you may prefer to weave in the contrasting yarn as shown on page 65.

You can work bobbles in as many different colours as you like.

Wrapping techniques

A variety of effects can be achieved by manipulating the yarn in different ways – wrapping it around your thumb to make a pile fabric; wrapping it around a group of stitches to draw then together and produce smocking; and wrapping it around the needle two or more times to create a line or area of openwork called a dropped stitch pattern.

Loop stitch

To produce a looped pile or shaggy fabric, wrap the yarn around the thumb at regular close intervals. For a shaggy effect, cut the resulting loops. This stitch is best suited to the right-hand method of holding the yarn, as shown on page 18. (Left-handed readers should reverse these images.)

Working loop stitch

Begin by working 2 rows of stocking/stockinette stitch, then knit one or two stitches for the selvedge.

1 Knit the next stitch, but do not let the original stitch slip off the needle. Bring the yarn forward between the needles and take it under the left thumb from back to front, making a loop of the desired length. The length of the loop can be increased by holding the thumb lower.

2 Knit again into the same stitch, and slip the original stitch off the LH needle, still keeping the thumb in the loop.

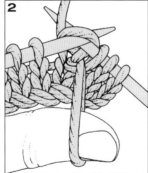

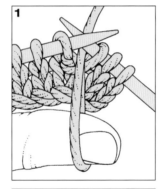

3 With the thumb still in the loop, insert the LH needle through the front of the 2 stitches just made, and knit both stitches together through the back. Slip the thumb out of the loop. Work to the position of the next loop, then repeat steps 1–3. In the drawing the loops are shown separated by a single knit stitch. They may be more widely spaced if desired.

4 Purl the next row. Slip the free needle through the loops, and pull them gently downwards.

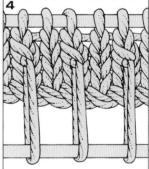

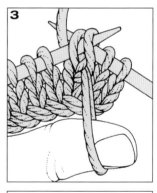

Smocking

You can produce a smocked fabric either by sewing a knitted fabric in a pattern (see page 72) or by knitting in the smocking as you go. The latter method, shown here, is based on a rib pattern, which you can vary by adjusting the thickness and/or spacing of the ribs.

Use a cable needle to group stitches together so that they can be wrapped with the yarn. You can wrap the grouped stitches before working them, as shown here, or you can work them first and then wrap them.

Basic ribbed smocking

Cast on a multiple of 8 stitches plus 10. Work in K2, P2 rib for 5 rows. On the 6th (right side) row, work the smocking, as follows:

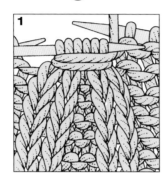

1 Purl the first 2 (purl) stitches. Slip the next 6 stitches on to the cable needle; hold them at front. Now wind the yarn twice around these stitches from left to right, pulling it firmly.

2 Knit 2, purl 2, knit 2 from the cable needle.

3 Now repeat steps 1 and 2 to the end.

4 Work in rib for 5 rows.

5 On the 12th row purl the first 2 stitches.

6 Slip 2 knit stitches on to the cable needle. Wind the yarn around these twice, knit them, then slip them off the cable needle.

7 Purl 2 stitches, repeat steps 2–4 to the last 2 stitches; knit 2. These 12 rows form the pattern.

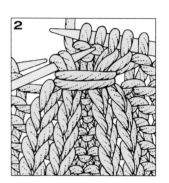

Dropped-stitch patterns

The technique shown here consists of elongating stitches to produce an open, ladder-like effect, either across the whole row or in small areas throughout the fabric. The yarn may be wrapped two or more times around the needle. This technique can be used as the basis of more elaborate patterns, such as elongated cross stitch.

Basic elongated stitch

1 Insert the RH needle knitwise into the stitch, take the yarn twice around the needle, and draw the 2 loops through the stitch, allowing it to slip off the needle. Repeat the step to the end of the row.

2 On the following row, purl into the first of each pair of loops and allow the extra loop to drop off the needle. You can use either side of the work as the right side. Produce longer stitches by winding the yarn 3 or more times around the needle.

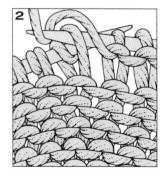

By now you will be confident in knitting back and forth in rows to produce flat pieces of fabric, which you then join to make a garment. Now is the time to look at the technique of knitting in rounds to produce a seamless fabric – either tubular or flat. You can use tubular fabrics in many ways: for ribbing around necklines; for socks, gloves and hats; and sometimes for the main body of a sweater. You can sew flat medallion shapes together to make a bedspread or use a large medallion to make a cushion cover or a shawl.

Knitting in the round

Circular/double-pointed needles

With the use of circular and double-pointed needles, you can achieve many different fabrics and finishing details that would be less satisfactory or even impossible if worked on conventional straight needles. By working in rounds on these needles, you can make a seamless, tubular fabric, to form the main part of a pullover, or a polo-neck collar; you can make leggings or socks, as well as berets and shawls.

Working in the round

Some knitting in the round is best done on a circular needle, some with double-pointed needles; some can be done with either. Whichever kind you are using, there are several points to remember. First of all, it is important to keep track of the beginning of each round. To do this, place a ring marker or a loop of contrasting yarn at the beginning of the round, and slip it onto the right-hand needle as you begin each new round. It may also be necessary to mark certain shaping points of pattern repeats in the same way.

When picking up stitches for working in the round – at a neckline, for example – the pattern will specify the correct number for the stitch pattern repeat. However, if you are altering a pattern in which this section is knitted flat, you may need to adjust the number of stitches to make sure you have an exact multiple of the repeat. For example, if you are working a K2, P2 rib, the total number of stitches must be divisible by 4; otherwise, the stitch pattern will not join up correctly.

Knitting with a circular needle

Of the two kinds of needle used for knitting in the round, the circular needle is easier to use. Only two needle points are involved in the work, and the bulk of the knitting slides easily between them as the work progresses. Also, there is only one join – as opposed to three or more if you are using double-pointed needles – so that it is easier to produce a smooth fabric. However, the circular needle cannot be used for small items, because the knitting needs to reach from one point of the needle to the other without stretching. The length of the needle used should be at least 5 cm (2 inches) less than the circumference of the piece of knitting.

If you have never used a circular needle, it's a good idea to practise using one for working in rows, as explained below. Some people prefer them to straight needles. And if you're knitting on a train or bus, they are less obtrusive to your seat companions. If you're changing from one kind to the other, make sure your tension remains the same.

Before beginning to work with a new circular needle or one that has been coiled up in its package for some time, straighten it by soaking it for about 15 minutes in warm water then pulling it gently through your fingers.

Working in rows with a circular needle

A circular needle is useful for working in rows. The weight of the work is distributed equally along the needle, which is ideal for large, heavy pieces, which can be tiring to work on a pair of ordinary needles.

To use a circular needle in this way, cast on in the chosen method. Work the first row beginning with the last cast-on stitch, rather than the first one, as in tubular knitting. At the end of the row, turn the needle so that the point with the last-worked stitch is in your left hand, and work the next row.

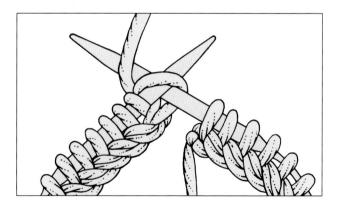

Tubular knitting on a circular needle

1 Cast on the required number of stitches. If you are using a single-needle method of casting on, wind an elastic band around one end to prevent the stitches from slipping off. Before beginning to knit, make sure that the stitches reach easily from one point to the other. Hold the needle so that the end with the last cast-on stitch is in your right hand and the end with the first cast-on stitch is in your left hand. Make sure that the stitches are not twisted on the needle; their lower edges should lie towards the centre of the ring. Now place a ring marker or a loop of contrasting yarn over the RH point, and insert the point into the first stitch on the LH needle.

2 Work the first stitch, pulling the yarn firmly to prevent a gap at the join.

3 Work the first (right-side) round of the specified pattern around to the marker. Slip the marker and continue with the second round of the pattern. Continue working in the chosen pattern as set. Cast/bind off in the usual way. After drawing the thread through the last stitch, take it through the first stitch of the round.

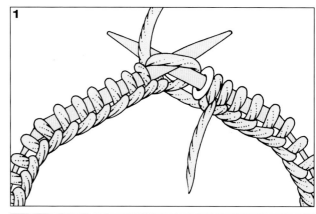

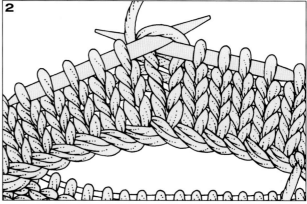

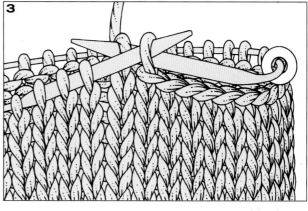

These socks are worked on double-pointed needles (see page 52).

Knitting with double-pointed needles

Double-pointed needles are sold in sets of four or five. A set of four is shown in these illustrations, but the principle is the same when using five. These needles are most often used for tubular knitting where there are too few stitches for even the shortest circular needle – for example, to work a seamless polo-neck collar on a sweater. The pattern may specify how many stitches are to be picked up; if not, you can either divide the number of stitches evenly or base the division on the shape of the work. For example, you might divide a V-neck into right front, left front and back, with a needle for each. The basic technique of picking up the stitches is the same as shown on page 33.

TIP

When resuming work on a piece of knitting on double-pointed needles, undo two or three stitches and work them again. They will have stretched slightly, and the interruption might be noticeable. The same applies to knitting worked in rows on ordinary needles, if you have had to stop in the middle of a row.

Tubular knitting on double-pointed needles

These instructions relate to a piece of knitting worked entirely in the round, from the cast-on stitches onwards. Step 3 relates also to working tubular knitting on picked-up stitches.

1 Begin by casting the required number of stitches on to a single-pointed needle of the same size as the double-pointed needles. Slip the stitches on to the double-pointed needles, leaving one needle free for working the stitches. Here, three needles out of a set of four are used.

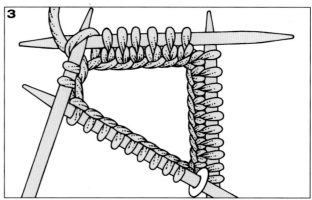

2 Arrange the needles so that their points cross as shown. Check to make sure that the stitches are not twisted. Place a ring marker over the point holding the last cast-on stitch. With the remaining needle, knit the first cast-on stitch; draw the yarn firmly to close the gap.

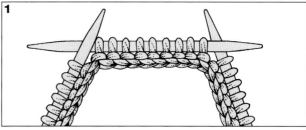

3 Continue working into all the stitches on the first needle. When this needle is free, use it to work into the stitches on the second needle. Continue in this way, taking care to pull the yarn firmly when working the first stitch on the new needle and slipping the marker at the beginning of each new round. When the work is the required depth, cast/bind off as usual. Draw the yarn through the first stitch of the round to make a neat join.

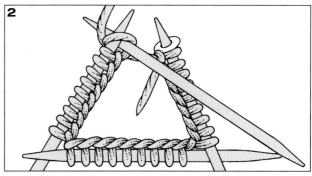

Medallions

By working in rounds, and increasing in a regular sequence, it is possible to make a variety of medallion shapes, useful for bonnets, berets and bedspreads. Using double-pointed needles, you work from the centre outwards (it is also possible to work from the outer edge inwards, decreasing rather than increasing). If you work the increases at the same point on every round, they form a pattern of straight lines radiating out from the centre. If you move them, you produce a swirl pattern. The type of increase you work also affects the appearance of the medallions. Bar increases produce an embossed effect, and 'make 1' increases and lifted increases produce a more subtle pattern (see pages 28–29). For a decorative effect, use an openwork increase.

Crocheted foundation

You may find this method of beginning a medallion easier than the cast-on method, especially where there are only 8 stitches in the first round.

Crochet a chain (see page 77) consisting of 8 stitches. Join the first and last chain with a slip stitch. Using 4 double-pointed needles, pick up 1 stitch through each chain (drawing the first loop through the chain and the loop that was on the hook as shown). Insert the needle through the top of each chain as shown. Place 2 stitches on each of the four needles.

Working a square medallion

Cast 8 stitches on to a double-pointed needle using the cable method (see page 16).

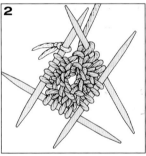

1 Arrange the stitches on 4 needles, as shown, and tie a thread marker at the beginning of the round – just before the last cast-on stitch.

2 Round 1 Using the fifth needle, knit into the back of every stitch. **Round 2** Knit into the front and back of every stitch: 16 stitches on the needles.

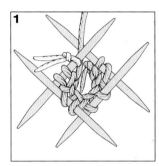

3 Round 3 Knit every stitch in the normal way. **Round 4** Knit into the front and back of the first stitch, knit 1, knit into the front and back of the third stitch, knit 1. Repeat on the remaining 3 sets of 4 stitches: 24 stitches. Placing each increase bar one stitch in from the corner, repeat rounds 3 and 4 until the medallion is the desired size. Cast/bind off.

Turning a heel

Socks are nearly always worked in the round, on double-pointed needles, in order to avoid the discomfort of a seam. The only complicated shaping involved is turning the heel, but even this is less difficult than it first appears. There are several basic methods of turning a heel; the one described here is called a Dutch heel. The shaping involves a technique known as short-row shaping, in which you hold some stitches on the needle while working others. In turning a heel you gradually decrease the held stitches and incorporate them into the centre section of the heel. You then rejoin the heel to the instep stitches. The main part of a sock is normally worked in stocking/ stockinette stitch. Single ribbing is the usual choice for the upper edge of the sock. Take care to cast on loosely so that the edge will not be uncomfortably tight.

1 Using a set of 4 double-pointed needles, cast on the specified number of stitches for the sock. The number should be divisible by 3 and also – if you are working in K1, P1 rib – by 2. Here the number is 42. Work in single rib (or other rib pattern) for the required length down to the top of the heel. Break off the yarn.

2 Now divide the heel stitches from those that will be used for the instep. The respective numbers will vary according to the pattern and the size; here, 22 stitches are used for the heel. Slip the first 11 stitches of the round and the last 11 on to one double-pointed needle. Slip the remaining instep stitches on to a spare needle; a short circular needle is convenient for this, as it holds the stitches in a curve, out of the way.

3 Rejoin the yarn to the RH edge of the heel stitches. Work in rows, in stocking/ stockinette stitch, until the heel is the required depth from ankle to bottom of heel, ending with a purl row.

4 On the next row, work across the first 14 stitches (the number will vary with the pattern, but should be approximately two thirds of the total), then decrease 1 stitch as follows: sl 1, K1, psso. Turn, leaving the remaining stitches unworked. There are 15 stitches on the needle.

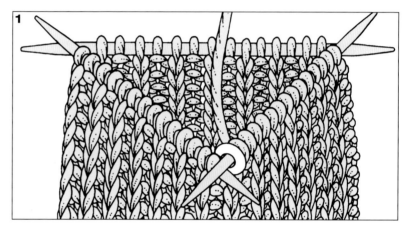

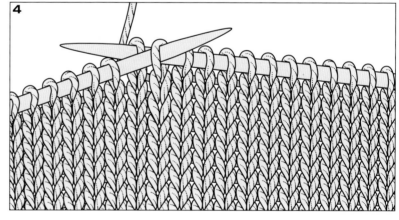

5 Purl across the first 7 stitches, then decrease 1 stitch: P2tog. Turn, leaving the remaining stitches unworked. Continue working on the centre stitches; at the end of every row work in 1 of the held stitches, at the same time decreasing 1 stitch. On knit rows decrease as in step 4; on purl rows, decrease as in step 5. Continue in this way until there are 8 stitches on the needle (that is, when all the held stitches have been decreased), ending with a wrong-side row.

6 Resume working in rounds on the 3 double-pointed needles. Work across the heel stitches, then pick up and knit the specified number along the left side of the heel; here it is 10 stitches. Using a second needle, work across the instep stitches. Using a third needle, pick up 10 stitches (or the specified number) along the right side of the heel, then knit across half of the heel stitches. Place a marker at this point to indicate the beginning of the round. At this point there are 48 stitches on the needles.

7 Work one round straight. Begin to decrease the stitches to either side of the instep: work to the last 3 stitches on the first needle, K2tog, work across the instep stitches, work the first stitch on third needle, then sl 1, K1, psso, work to the end.

8 Repeat this decrease round until the specified number of stitches remain on the needles. The sock is then worked straight until the toe shaping.

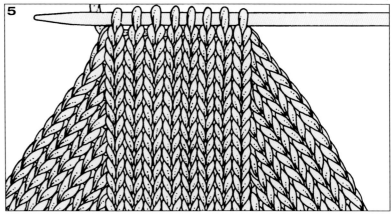
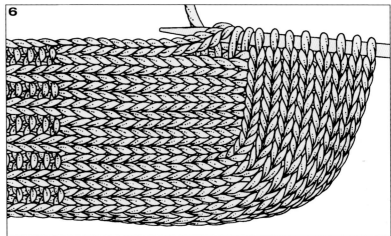

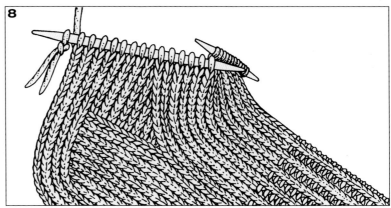

Shaping a gusset

A traditional Guernsey sweater is knitted mainly in the round. Even the sleeves are worked in this way, on stitches picked up from the yoke. The shaping incorporates an underarm gusset, which helps to make the garment comfortable. Although a gusset can be worked separately and sewn in, it is not difficult to knit one in as shown here, while working in the round. The garment is worked in the round up to the armpit. To indicate the side 'seams', purl a single stitch at these points on each round. At the widest part of the gusset the tubular knitting is interrupted and the front and back completed separately, working in rows. Then stitches are picked up for the sleeves and the tubular knitting recommenced. The gusset stitches are decreased down to a single purled stitch for the sleeve 'seam'.

1 To begin shaping the gusset, increase 1 stitch on either side of the 'seam' by working a 'make 1' increase (see page 29) just before the purled stitch, knitting the stitch, then increasing again just after it.

2 On the next round, purl across all stitches.

3 On the next round, work up to the 3 gusset stitches, make 1, work across gusset, make 1. Continue in this way, adding 2 stitches to the gusset on alternate rounds, until it is the desired width. Work one round straight; slip the gusset stitches on to a stitch holder.

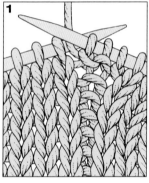

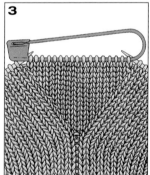

4 Complete the front and back sections separately. Join the shoulder seams.

5 Using a set of double-pointed needles, knit across the gusset stitches, then pick up and knit the stitches for the sleeve from the front and back of the garment.

6 Work the sleeve downwards, decreasing on either side of the gusset. On the first round: Sl 1, K1, psso, K to last 2 gusset sts, K2tog. Work the next round without decreasing.

7 Continue to decrease 2 stitches on alternate rounds until 1 stitch remains in the gusset. This stitch marks the sleeve 'seam'; purl it on every round.

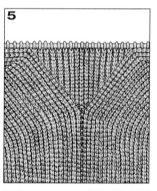

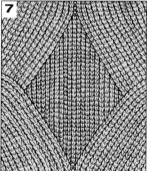

Joining in new yarn

You should not need to join in yarn mid-row when working in rows, but this cannot be avoided in circular knitting. Join in at an inconspicuous place if the fabric is smooth. On textured fabric it may be possible to join in yarn anywhere in the round.

Double strand method

Use this method if the yarn is fuzzy and the stitch pattern is a textured one. The first stitch in the new yarn should be a knit stitch.

1 Having worked the last stitch in the old yarn, let this yarn drop down on the wrong side of the work. Turn back the end of the new yarn for 10cm (4in). Insert the needle into the next stitch and draw through the loop of the new yarn, to form the first stitch in the new yarn.

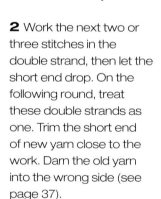

2 Work the next two or three stitches in the double strand, then let the short end drop. On the following round, treat these double strands as one. Trim the short end of new yarn close to the work. Darn the old yarn into the wrong side (see page 37).

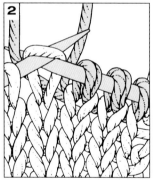

Threading-in method

This method is preferred when working stocking/stockinette stitch in a smooth yarn. Thread the end of the new yarn into a yarn needle. Take it through the old yarn for about 4cm (1½in). Continue knitting, and work in the joined yarn. Trim the loose ends later.

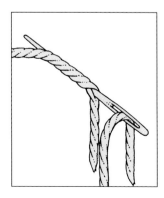

Stitch patterns in rounds

Instructions for stitch patterns are normally given for working in rows. This might put you off working in the round, thinking that you will be able to use only the basic stitches.

Happily, however, you can easily convert many stitch patterns for working in the round. As already noted (see page 50), you produce stocking/stockinette stitch by knitting every round. Conversely, reverse stocking/stockinette stitch results if your purl every round. For garter stitch, you knit and purl alternate rounds. For most rib patterns, you simply knit and purl the same stitches on every round. The principle, therefore, is that any stitch you normally purl on a wrong-side row should now be knitted when you work on the right side, and vice versa.

This means that any stitch pattern in which you simply purl every wrong-side row can easily be worked in the round by knitting all these rows.

If you wish to use a more complex stitch pattern, you may first need to work a sample in rows, until you become familiar with its construction. Then write your own revised instructions and work a sample in the round. Remember when working in the round, however, to omit the edge stitches.

Try working this simple stitch in rounds (see page 168).

There are many ways of combining two or more colours in a piece of knitting – some complex, some extremely simple – all capable of producing rich and exciting effects. They include simple horizontal stripes, fascinating slipstitch patterns, jacquard motifs and traditional Fair Isle designs.

Many commercially produced patterns include colourwork; but it is also possible to add a colour pattern to a one-colour design, thereby giving it your own personal stamp of individuality.

Colourwork

Horizontal stripes

You can create many effects simply by working rows in different colours to produce stripes. The simplest version is a two-colour stripe, where you change the colours after a regular number of rows. Worked in stocking/stockinette stitch, this has a neat, crisp appearance. You can achieve more subtle effects by using shades of the same colour; by varying the number of rows worked, in a regular or random pattern; by using the purled side of the work, giving the colour changes a broken appearance; or by introducing the occasional purled row on the right side of a stocking/stockinette stitch fabric for textural interest. Horizontal stripes need not run horizontally. If you work the garment from one side edge to the other the stripes will run vertically. (You can achieve true vertical stripes by using one of the methods shown on pages 62–63.)

Joining new colours

1 Tie the new colour to the old one at the RH edge of the work, using a double knot. Do not cut off the old yarn.

2 Continue knitting with the new yarn. On every second row twist the two yarns around each other to help keep the edge neat. When changing back to the first colour, bring it in front of the second colour. Avoid pulling it tightly when beginning to knit with the new yarn.

If the yarn is fine, up to three colours can be carried up the side in this way. Where more colours are used, or where one colour is not used for many rows, they should be cut off and rejoined as required. This is also necessary, of course, where new colours are introduced on wrong-side rows and so joined at the LH edge.

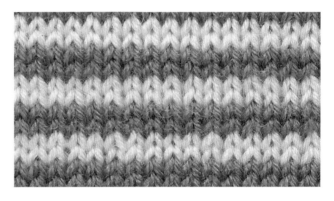

You can work horizontal stripes simply by changing colour at the side edge. Here the colours have been changed after every second row.

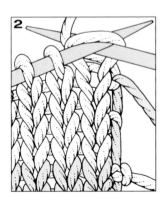

Chevron stripes have been created here by working a chevron stitch pattern and changing colour as for ordinary horizontal stripes.

Slipstitch colour patterns

Slipstitch colour patterns use one colour in a row and achieve a blended colour effect by slipping stitches, so that the colour from the previous row encroaches upon the row being worked. The working yarn is loosely carried behind the slipped stitches. In some patterns the stitches draw in, so that more stitches are needed for a given width. It is important to make a good-sized tension/gauge swatch if you substitute a slipstitch pattern for another stitch. The stitches slipped in these patterns are always slipped purlwise. Instructions 'with yarn at front' and 'with yarn at back' refer to the back and front in relation to the knitter; not the right and wrong sides of the work. You take the yarn directly to the front or back and not over the needle. Having slipped the stitches, the yarn is at the back if the next stitch is a knit stitch or the front if it is a purl stitch.

Basic slipstitch technique

The simple pattern shown here – called tricolour wave stripe – will introduce you to the principles of working slipstitch colour patterns.

1 First cast on a multiple of 4 stitches plus 1, using colour A.
Row 1 P one row.
Row 2 (RS) With B, K1, *with yarn at back sl 3 purlwise, K1, rep from * to end.

2 Row 3 With B, P2, *with yarn at front sl 1, P3, rep from * to last 3 sts, sl 1, P2.
Row 4 With B, K to end. **Row 5** With B, P to end. **Rows 6–9** With C, rep Rows 2–5.
Rows 10–13 With A, rep Rows 2–5.

The right side of tricolour wave stripe illustrates the construction of a typical slipstitch colour pattern.

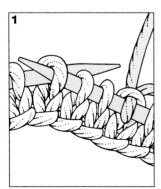
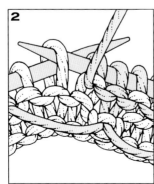

The reverse side of tricolour wave stripe demonstrates how yarn is carried from one stitch to another.

Vertical colour changes

You can work patterns with more than one colour in a row using one of several methods: carrying, or 'stranding', the unused colour loosely along the back of the work until it is needed again; 'weaving' the unused yarn into the work at intervals, or with every alternate stitch, until it is needed; and working with several different balls of yarn, positioned across the work and picked up as required – a method called the 'intarsia' technique. The method you choose is often dictated by the type of design, but also by the weight and colour of the yarn you are using. For example, you would normally knit a repeating-motif pattern, such as a Fair Isle design that uses only two colours in any one row, using the stranding method and incorporating weaving where the unused yarn must span long distances. Weaving is better suited to 'busy' patterns.

Intarsia technique

The intarsia technique might be used for a design that includes more than two colours in a row, because carrying more than two colours across every row would make the work too bulky. You might also use the intarsia technique for designs with wide vertical or diagonal stripes, with, say, 10 stitches in each stripe, because where the stranding method would leave long strands of yarn – likely to be snagged – on the wrong side, and weaving in the yarn might leave noticeable marks on the right side, and for large repeating motifs, individual motifs and pictorial knitting.

The first step is to prepare the yarn by winding it on to bobbins. These do not unroll as balls of yarn do, and so are less likely to become tangled. It is possible to buy plastic bobbins at some yarn shops; however, if the yarn you are using is thick, you may prefer to make your own bobbins of the desired size from pieces of cardboard.

Motifs designed to be worked using the intarsia method can sometimes be more easily worked in Swiss darning (see page 70).

In the illustrations opposite the fabric being worked is stocking/stockinette stitch; in the case of reverse stocking/stockinette stitch you hold the yarns on the knit side of the work. The process of twisting the yarns is essentially the same: take the old yarn over the new yarn, then bring it up in the correct position to work.

Making a bobbin

Cut a cardboard rectangle of the desired size. For thick yarns, about 5 by 8cm (2 by 3½in) will do. In each short end, cut notches as shown. Wind the yarn through the notches.

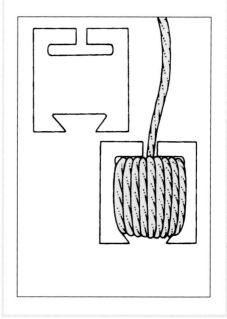

Changing colour on a knit row

Work in the first colour to the point for the colour change. If the second colour is being introduced for the first time, tie it to the first colour. On subsequent rows the procedure is as follows:

Drop the first colour over the second, pick up the second colour and continue knitting with it. In this way, the yarns are twisted around each other. If this were not done, the two areas of colour would be separate, leaving a split in the fabric.

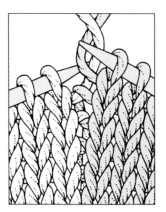

Changing colour on a purl row

Work in the first colour to the point for the colour change. Drop the first colour over the second, pick up the second and continue purling with it. On both knit and purl rows, work the stitches before and after the change fairly tightly to avoid leaving a gap.

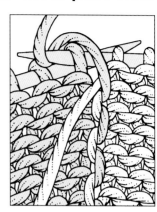

This is the wrong side of the intarsia work, showing the two colours twisting around each other where they are joined together.

Stranding yarns

Stranding is the basic technique used when knitting a repeating motif using two colours that are alternated at short intervals. As a general rule you should not strand yarns across more than five stitches; otherwise the elasticity of the work is likely to be impaired. Where you must carry yarn for more than five stitches, you should weave it into the work, using the technique shown on page 65. Both stranding and weaving are easier to do on knit rows than on purl rows, and when working in rounds. Whether you work in rounds or in rows, it is important to hold the unused yarn loosely in order to avoid puckering the fabric. For a smooth tension/gauge it is best to hold one yarn in each hand, combining the right-hand and the left-hand methods.

Stranding yarn on a knit row

1 On the row in which the second colour is introduced, join it at the RH edge. Begin knitting in the colour specified by the pattern, carrying the other colour loosely across the back of the work. To knit with the RH yarn, hold the LH yarn slightly under the needles.

2 To knit with the LH yarn, hold the RH yarn out of the way.

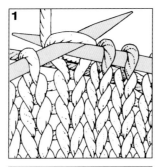

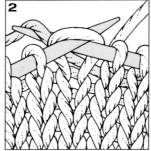

Stranding yarn on a purl row

Here the process is the same as for a knit row except that the stranded yarn is held at the front of the work.

1 To purl with the RH yarn, hold the LH yarn under the needles.

2 To purl with the LH yarn, hold the RH yarn out of the way.

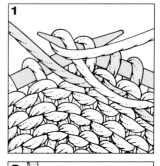

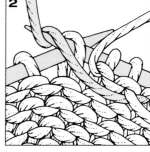

The best way of working an Argyle pattern is to hold one colour in each hand, as shown, knitting with them alternately and stranding or weaving the unused colour on the wrong side of the work.

Weaving yarns

In weaving, you occasionally catch unused yarn into a stitch. You can do this on every alternate stitch to produce a dense fabric with no loose strands on the wrong side. Or you can do it every few stitches. Avoid working the yarn into stitches directly above each other, as this may cause a visible indentation in the fabric.

Knitting – weaving in LH yarn

When knitting with the RH yarn, take the LH yarn alternately below and above the stitches.

To weave the LH yarn below, simply hold it under the work as if for stranding (see page 64).

To weave the LH yarn above, take it over the RH needle. Take the RH yarn around the needle to knit; draw this loop through the stitch.

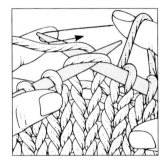

Purling – weaving in LH yarn

When purling with the RH yarn, take the LH yarn alternately below and above the stitches.

To weave the LH yarn below, simply hold it away from the work as if for stranding (see page 64).

To weave the LH yarn above, take it over the RH needle (but not all the way around it), and purl (left) with the RH yarn.

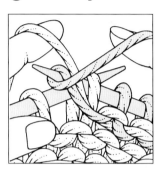

Knitting – weaving in RH yarn

To weave the RH yarn above, simply hold it away from the work as if for stranding (see page 64) and knit with the LH yarn. To take the RH yarn below:

1 Bring the RH yarn around the needle as if to knit.

2 Bring the LH yarn around the needle as if to knit.

3 Reverse the RH yarn, taking it to the left and under the needle point – and thus off the needle.

4 Complete the stitch in the LH yarn.

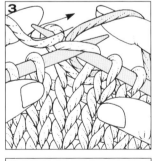

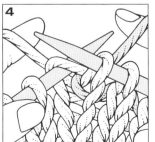

Purling – weaving in RH yarn

To weave the RH yarn above, simply hold it away from the work as if for stranding (see page 64), and purl with the LH yarn. To weave the RH yarn below:

1 Loop the RH yarn around the needle as shown.

2 Bring the LH yarn over the needle as if to purl.

3 Reverse the RH yarn, taking it to the left and under the needle point – and thus off the needle.

4 Complete the stitch in the LH yarn.

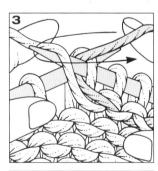

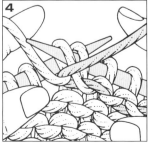

Following a chart

Individual and repeating motifs for colour patterns are often given in the form of a chart, which is easier to follow than written instructions. The colours may be shown on the chart, or they may be represented by symbols, with an accompanying key. Each square on the chart represents a single stitch. You work a chart from bottom to top. Right-side rows are normally given odd numbers, which you work from right to left. You work the even-numbered, wrong-side rows from left to right. This rule does not apply to working in rounds (see page 50) in which you knit all the rows from right to left. Charts for repeating motifs normally include only the one repeat, along with any edge stitches required. The repeat itself is marked off with a heavy line; where several sizes are given there may be additional edge stitches given for the larger sizes.

Intarsia chart

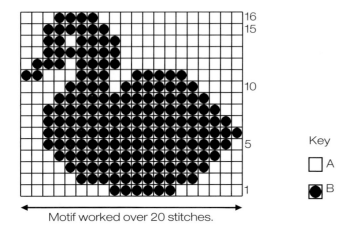

Key

☐ A

● B

Motif worked over 20 stitches.

The simple chart above is for an individual duck motif. Only one contrasting colour is used, represented by a dot. Only every fifth row is marked on the chart, plus the final 16th row.

Fair Isle chart

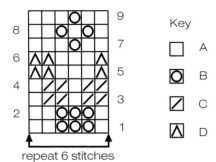

repeat 6 stitches

Key

☐ A

Ⓞ B

⊘ C

⟋\ D

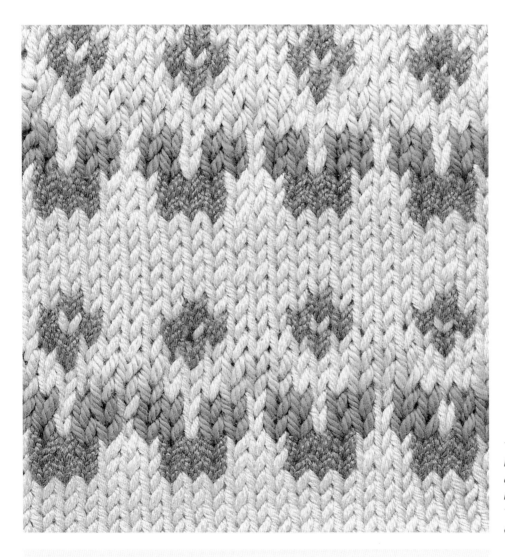

The slightly more complicated Fair Isle pattern uses three contrasting colours. Every row on the chart is marked. The pattern repeat is worked over 6 stitches.

TIP

When following a chart, it is important to keep careful track of your progress. A good way of doing this is to photocopy the chart and draw a line through each row as you complete it. If the chart is small, enlarging it at the same time will make it easier to follow.

Knitting is often embellished in some way. There may be a twisted cord around a waistline or at a neck, or the front opening of a cardigan might have a crocheted edging. Perhaps you will work beads, sequins or embroidery stitches into your knitting, or add a deep fringe to a shawl to help it hang gracefully. Conversely, you can use knitting itself as the embellishment, in the form of a lacy knitted edging. In the following few pages you will find instructions for all of these techniques.

Embellishments

Embroidery on knitting

You can use embroidery stitches to add motifs to a piece of plain knitting or to enhance or accentuate a stitch pattern. The most common embroidery technique used in knitting is Swiss darning. This is worked on a stocking/stockinette stitch fabric and gives the appearance of having been knitted in. Motifs for Swiss darning are normally given in chart form, with one square of the chart representing each stitch. You can also use a cross-stitch technique in the same way. Embroidery on knitting is always worked with a blunt-ended yarn needle to avoid splitting the yarn. You can use a knitting yarn or embroidery thread; the only criterion is that the thread should be appropriate in weight and texture for the background and to the technique used. It is important to stitch with an easy tension to preserve the elasticity of the fabric.

Swiss darning

Use a single strand of yarn, the same weight and type as that used for the knitting. Begin at the bottom RH corner of the motif, and secure the yarn with one or two stitches at the back of the area to be covered with the embroidery. Bring the needle up through the base of the first stitch to be embroidered.

1 Take the needle up to the right, along over the stitch, then under it from right to left, bringing it out as shown in the upper left of the drawing.

2 Take the needle down at the centre of the stitch, where it emerged, and then one stitch to the left as shown in the lower left of the drawing. Repeat steps 1 and 2 to cover this and all subsequent stitches. Take care not to pull the stitches tightly.

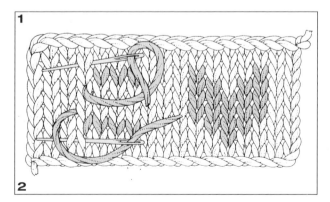

Cross stitch

This stitch, too, is well suited to a stocking/stockinette stitch fabric. The yarn used should be somewhat thinner than that used for the knitting. Depending on the scale of the work, it is best to work over groups of four stitches. Secure the yarn to the wrong side.

1 Bring the needle up at the lower RH corner of the area to be covered with the stitch, and take it down at the upper LH.

2 Bring it up at the lower LH corner and take it down at the upper RH corner. This completes the stitch.

3 When working cross stitch it is important that all the lower stitches slant in one direction and all the top stitches in another. Therefore, it is better to work in rows, in two stages.

Chain stitch

You can use this versatile stitch to work lines in any direction. Varying the thickness of yarn and the spacing of stitches produces quite different effects.

1 Bring the needle up to the right side of the work, form the thread into a small loop, and take the needle back down into the fabric and up inside the loop (top). Pull the thread gently to tighten the loop. Continue forming loops in this way along the line of stitching. Secure the last loop by taking the needle down into the fabric just outside the loop (bottom).

2 You can work individual chain stitches in a circle to suggest the petals of a flower; in this form the stitch is called 'lazy daisy'. You can also scatter them over the surface.

This picture shows lazy daisy stitches being worked.

French knots

It is usually better to choose a yarn at least as thick as that used for the knitting, so that the knots will stand out prominently on the surface.

Bring the needle up at the point for the knot. Then, holding the yarn taut, wrap it once around the needle, close to the place where it emerged. Now take the needle to the wrong side, just beside the starting point.

Always take the needle through quickly, so the thread does not have a chance to unwind. For a larger knot, take the thread twice around the needle.

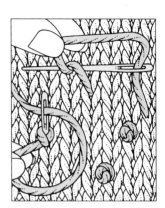

Buttonhole and blanket stitches

These stitches are useful as well as decorative. Worked in the same way, the stitches are called 'blanket' when they are spaced apart and 'buttonhole' when they are worked close together.

1 Work from left to right. Take the needle to the right, to the desired width of the blanket stitch, then insert it above this point at the desired depth (top). Loop the thread around to the right and bring the needle up over it on the lower stitching line. This completes the stitch. Continue working to the right in this way. Secure the last loop as shown.

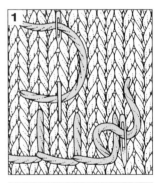

2 You can also work buttonhole stitch in circles to produce stylized flower shapes.

Couching

Use this stitch to decorate a knitted fabric with threads that would be difficult or impossible to sew through the fabric. Use a fine sewing thread for the stitching.

1 Lay the main thread on top of the knitting, leaving a short end free. Bring the stitching thread to the right side, a little beyond the point where the couched thread will be fastened. Take it over the couched thread and back into the fabric.

2 Make another stitch about 1cm (½in) further along the stitching line. Continue in this way. After the last stitch, fasten the working thread on the wrong side.

3 Use a blunt-ended yarn needle to take each end of the couched thread to the wrong side. Using fine thread, sew the ends in place.

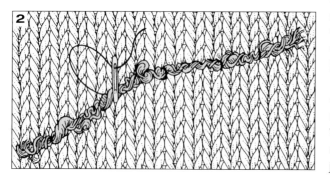

Smocking

As an alternative to knitting in smocking (see page 46), you can embroider the smocking on a knitted fabric. The yarn used for the smocking can be the knitting yarn or an embroidery thread. Work the fabric in a K1, P3 rib.

1 Secure the smocking thread at the lower RH corner, to the left of the second rib.

2 Take the thread back over the first rib and up again at the starting point, drawing the two ribs together.

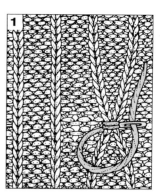

3 Work 2 more back-stitches over the ribs, then take the thread under the work and bring it up to the left of the fourth rib.

4 Join the third and fourth ribs in the same way. Work to the end. Work the next row above the first, joining different ribs.

This knitted toy monkey's mouth has been couched in place, giving him a smoother smile than if it had been embroidered.

Decorative cords

You can use several kinds of decorative cord for drawstrings or decorative ties at a neckline, for example. Experiment with these different kinds of cord, using different types of yarn, to discover their possibilities.

Plaited cord

Cut the strands slightly longer than the required finished length of the cord, making sure that the number of strands is divisible by 3. Knot the strands together at one end, and pin the knot to a fixed object, such as the upholstered arm of a chair. Plait the strands. Knot the other end and trim the ends.

Knitted cord

For this cord you need two double-pointed needles. You only use one strand of yarn, working with the end of yarn still attached to the ball.

1 Cast on 2 stitches and knit them in the usual way. Without turning the work, move the stitches towards the other end of the needle, bring the yarn firmly from left to right, behind the work, and knit the two stitches.

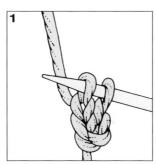

2 Continue in this way until the cord is the required length. Knit the two stitches together and fasten off. You can sew the loose yarn ends into the cord, or use them to attach a pompom, tassel or bead to each end.

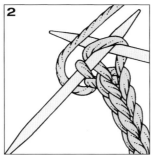

Twisted cord

The important thing to remember when making this cord is to twist the strands very tightly, otherwise the finished cord will be flimsy. To estimate how many strands you will need, cut several short strands, twist them together, and then double this twisted length; you can then add or subtract strands as appropriate. Cut the strands for the cord so that they are three times the finished length.

1 Knot the strands together at one end, and anchor this end to a fixed object, such as a doorknob; or ask someone to help you turn from that end.

2 Tie the strands together at the other end, and slip a pencil through the knot.

3 Holding the strands taut, turn the pencil clockwise, continuing to turn until the strands kink up in several places if the tension is relaxed.

4 Bring the two knotted ends together, and give the cord a firm shake; it will twist around itself. Smooth out the coils, and tie a knot a short distance from the folded end. Also knot the two free ends together. Trim both ends and fluff them out.

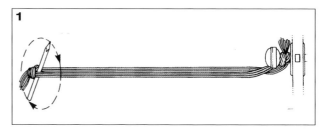

Trimmings

You can decorate many kinds of knitted garment with fringes, tassels or pompoms. A simple fringe is the perfect finishing touch for a scarf; a more elaborate knotted one makes an elegant edging on a shawl. Pompoms make perky trimmings for hats and are a favourite on children's clothes. You can sew a tassel to the ends of knitted cords or attach one to each of the four corners of a knitted (or woven fabric) cushion cover.

Simple fringe

This fringe is essentially a series of tassels. Ideally, the strands for each tassel should be about two and a half times the finished length.

1 Fold the group of strands in half. With the help of a crochet hook, draw the folded end through the edge from front to back.

2 Bring the strands through the loop, and pull downwards gently, bringing the loop up to the edge.

This scarf has been finished with a simple fringe.

Knotted fringe

You can create elegant lattice-like effects with this technique. The fringe should be at least 12cm (4½in) deep; it uses fewer strands than a simple fringe.

1 Knot the strands into the edge of the fabric as for a simple fringe, placing them slightly further apart.

2 When you have attached all the strands, take half the strands from the first group at one edge and half from the next group, and tie them together as shown. Join the remaining strands from the second group to half the strands from the third group. Continue to the end.

3 On the second row tie the separated strands together. You can add more rows of knotting if you like. An attractive variation is to join some strands with beads.

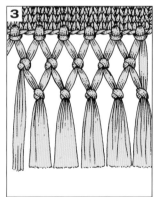

Pompoms

To make a pompom, first cut two identical circles from thin cardboard, the diameter of the finished pompom. In the centre of the circles draw another circle, one quarter the diameter of the outer circle. Now cut the centre circle out of each larger circle using a pair of sharp scissors.

1 Cut a long length of yarn, thread it into a blunt-ended yarn needle, and wrap the yarn around the two circles as shown. Add more yarn until the hole is tightly filled.

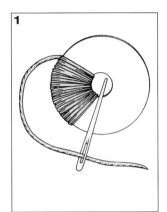

2 With sharp scissors cut around the edge of the circles. Pull the cardboard circles apart slightly and tie a length of yarn firmly around the strands in the middle. Cut away the cardboard circles. Trim any uneven strands.

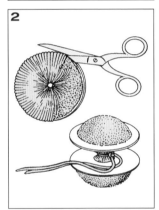

Pompoms attached to plaited cords make a cheerful trim for this hat.

Tassels

From stiff cardboard cut a rectangle the length of the finished tassel.

1 Wind the yarn around the cardboard until the tassel is the desired thickness. Loop a piece of yarn under the strands at one end. Cut through the other end.

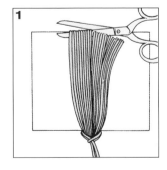

2 Make a loop at one end of a length of yarn; holding the loop alongside the strands, wind the other end around the strands several times. Now slip the free end through the loop. Pull on the two ends to fasten them; trim the ends and push them inside the wound yarn.

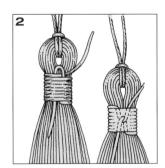

Beads and sequins

For a design that uses many beads or sequins, you should knit them in using one of the following methods. The simpler of the two is the slipstitch method, while the yarn-around-needle method must be used when working beads into consecutive stitches. Keeping the beads on the right side of the work requires a little more skill here, than in the slipstitch method. You can work them into the knit side or purl side of the work. On the wrong side, work fairly tightly to hold the heads in place.

Threading beads on to yarn

First thread a sewing needle with a double strand of strong thread as shown. Slip the end of the yarn through the loop of thread, and turn back the end. Thread the beads or sequins on to the yarn, always keeping one bead on the loop to hold it in place.

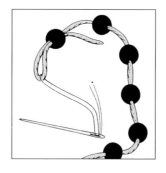

Yarn-around-needle method

1 On a right-side row, insert the needle through the back of the next stitch and push a bead up close to the work.

2 Take the yarn around the needle, and push the bead through the stitch to the front. Complete the stitch.

3 On a wrong-side row, insert the needle purlwise through the back of the loop. Push the bead through the loop.

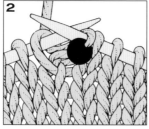

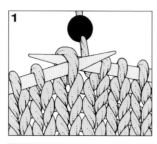

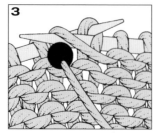

Slip stitch method

You can used this method wherever the beads or sequins are separated by at least one stitch. It is normally worked on right-side rows, but you can also work from the wrong side. Complete at least two rows of knitting before working the beads in.

1 Knit up to the position for the bead. Bring the yarn forward and slip the next stitch knitwise.

2 Push the bead up and knit the next stitch.

3 If working a wrong-side row, take the yarn back to the right side of the work and slip the next stitch purlwise. Push the bead up so that it lies close to the right side, and purl the next stitch.

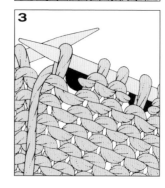

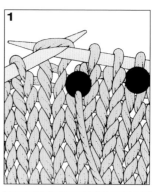

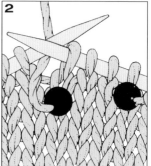

Crochet

Basic crochet techniques are useful for the knitter and are not difficult to learn. You only need one implement and mistakes are easily corrected; you simply unravel the work back to the mistake, slip the hook into the loop, and continue. You can use crochet to make simple button loops and to finish edges. It is also sometimes used for seams.

Working a chain
(abbreviated ch)

The chain is the basic crochet stitch. A given number of chain stitches are used to begin work and are the equivalent of casting on in knitting.

1 Begin with a slip knot. Leave the hook in the loop, and grasp the base of the knot with the left thumb and forefinger. Slide the hook forward under the tensioned yarn and turn it to catch the yarn as shown.

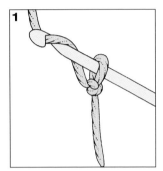

2 Keeping the yarn tensioned, pull the hook back through the loop to form a new loop. Repeat steps 1 and 2 to complete the chain to the right length.

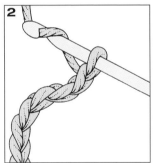

Double crochet
(abbreviated dc)

Work this stitch to provide a neat, firm edge on a completed knitted fabric, perhaps in a different colour.

1 Secure the yarn to the RH corner of the work. Insert the hook into the first stitch, front to back, and draw through a loop.

2 Take the yarn around the hook and draw this loop through the first loop.

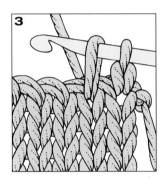

3 Insert the hook into the next stitch and draw through a second loop.

4 Take the yarn around the hook and draw it through both loops. One double crochet has been completed. Repeat steps 3 and 4 as required. To turn a corner, work 3 stitches into the corner stitch.

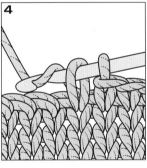

Slip stitch
(abbreviated sl st)

Use this stitch to join two pieces of knitting. Insert the hook through both layers. Draw a loop through the stitch and through the loop on the hook in one movement. Continue in this way along the seam.

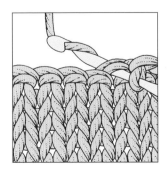

How to hold the hook and yarn is shown here. The yarn goes around the left little finger, under the second and third finger then over the first finger.

The skills covered here include some that you may need only occasionally, such as inserting a zip or working a knitted-in hem, as well as skills that will give your knitting a professional touch. These include such refinements as a bias cast-/bind-off for slanting shoulder seams, an invisible cast-on edge, how to join knitted edges by grafting rather than sewing them together and several different kinds of hems and pockets. As you gain experience and confidence as a knitter, you will often find that you can improve on the techniques specified in a commercial pattern. For example, you might wish to knit a patch pocket on picked-up stitches, rather than sew it on. Practise these special techniques and keep the samples for reference later.

Special techniques

Advanced casting on

The two methods of casting on shown here are worth learning. They are often called 'invisible' casting-on methods because they employ a separate length of yarn that is later removed. Method 1 is used on a single-rib fabric; when the foundation yarn is removed, the edge that remains appears to consist only of ribbing, although the first four rows are actually produced by a slipstitch technique. The smooth edge is flexible and attractive, and worth the small amount of extra work involved. In Method 2 the edge that remains consists of loose stitches that can either be picked up and knitted (for a lacy edging perhaps) or grafted to another edge for an invisible seam.

Invisible cast-on – method 1

Use this method for a single ribbing, worked over an odd number of stitches. Use a contrasting yarn (later removed) for the initial cast-on.

1 Using the thumb or double cast-on method (easier to remove than the cable method), cast on to the needle half the number of stitches required, rounding the result up to the next number. For example, if 53 stitches are needed, you should cast on 27 (rounded up from 26½).

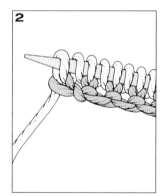

2 Join on the main yarn and cut off the contrasting yarn. Work the first 5 rows as follows:
Row 1 (inc row) K1, *yf, K1, rep from * to end. The correct number of stitches should now be on the needle.

3 Row 2 Wyf sl 1 purlwise, *K1, wyf sl 1 purlwise, rep from * to end.
Row 3 K1, *wyf sl 1 purlwise, K1, rep from * to end.
Row 4 Rep row 2.
Row 5 Rep row 3.

4 Now work in K1, P1 rib for the required depth, and unpick the contrasting yarn.

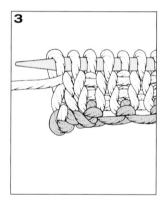

The edge produced by the invisible cast-on (Method 1) is flexible, attractive and hard-wearing.

Invisible cast-on – method 2

Use a contrasting yarn, of any colour, for this method; you will remove it later.

1 Make a slip knot in the main yarn (A) and place it on the needle. Tie the contrasting yarn (B) to the main yarn, and hold the two yarns in the left hand as shown. Take yarn A over the needle from front to back.

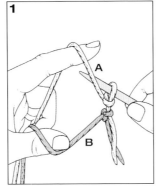

2 Take yarn B over the needle from back to front. The yarns should now be crossed on top of the needle.

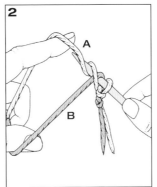

3 Take yarn A over the needle again from front to back, and pull both yarns around the far side of the needle, so bringing them below it. Recite to yourself, 'front to back, back to front, front to back and down'. The contrasting yarn should lie in a straight line along the lower edge of the cast-on stitches.

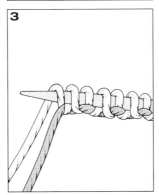

4 When you have cast on the required number of stitches, tie the contrasting yarn to the main yarn at the end, and cut it off. Leave this yarn in place until the knitting is completed, then remove it and pick up the stitches as instructed by the pattern for further knitting or grafting.

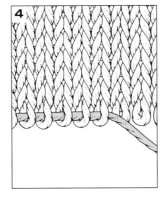

Multiple increase

Some patterns will require you to cast on a number of stitches at a side edge in order to work some shaping – for example to add a sleeve on a T-shaped garment. Any convenient cast-on method can be used for this; however, if you are using a two-strand method, such as the double cast-on, you will need to tie an extra strand on to the work.

If you are making an increase at the left-hand edge of the garment (that is, the left edge with the work facing you), you cast on the extra stitches immediately after completing a right-side row, so that the first row you work on them will be a wrong-side row. If the increase is to come at the right-hand edge, you cast on the stitches after completing a wrong-side row.

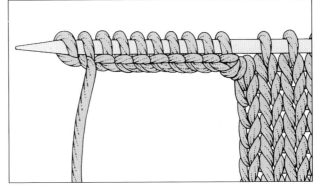

There is no shoulder seam on this cardigan. The sleeves were knitted as part of the garment, using a multiple increase (see pages 100–103)

Advanced casting/binding off

Here are four different ways of casting/binding off. The suspended cast-/bind-off is a more flexible than the basic method (see page 16). The bias cast-/bind-off is a special way of shaping an edge that would otherwise be cast/bound off on alternate rows, producing a stepped effect. The double cast-/bind-off can be used to join a shoulder seam or any straight edges with the same number of stitches. The invisible cast-/bind-off is ideal on a piece of single ribbing – where an inconspicuous finish is desired.

Suspended cast-/bind-off

You can use this method on ribbing (although the edge is somewhat more conspicuous than a rib cast-/bind-off) or on garments where elasticity is important.

1 Work the first 2 stitches. *Lift the first stitch over the second, as usual, but leave the lifted stitch on the LH needle.

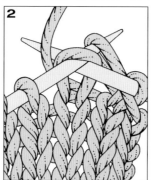

2 Still leaving the first 2 stitches in place, work the third stitch.

3 Drop the second and third stitches off the LH needle. Two loops are now on the RH needle. Repeat from * until 2 stitches remain; knit these together.

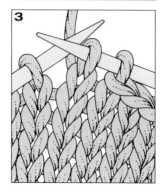

Bias cast-/bind-off

A pattern instructs you to cast/bind off in stages and gives the exact number of stitches to cast/bind off on each shaping row. The process takes 5 rows, typically. You can easily convert the instructions to make a bias cast-/bind-off. The LH edge is shown here.

1 Work up to the last row before the shoulder shaping, ending at the neck edge with a wrong-side row. Work across the stitches up to those to be cast/bound off. Turn, leaving these stitches unworked. Slip the first stitch purlwise.

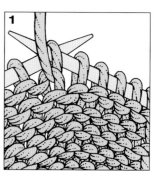

2 Work across to the end (neck edge). Turn and work across the stitches up to the next group to be cast/bound off. Turn, leaving these stitches unworked. Slip the first stitch purlwise. Work across to the end. Continue until only the last group of stitches remains to be worked. With right side facing, cast/bind off all stitches.

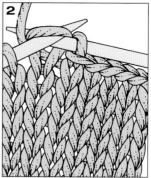

3 The cast-/bound-off edge slopes smoothly. To cast/bind off a RH edge, work as above, reversing the terms 'right side' and 'wrong side'.

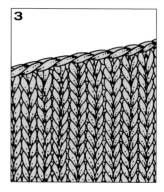

Double cast-/bind-off

This is a combined cast-/bind-off and seam, and makes a good finish to a bias cast-/bind-off. The edges to be joined must have the same number of stitches.

Work the two pieces of knitting up to the last row before casting/binding off; leave the stitches on a spare needle.

Before working the cast-/bind-off, arrange the two pieces on the needles so that when they are placed together with right sides facing the needles will point towards the right.

1 Holding the two pieces together, with right sides facing, insert a third needle knitwise through the first stitch on both pieces, and knit the 2 together. Work the next 2 stitches together in the same way.

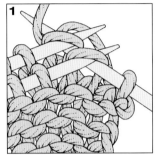

2 Using one of the two needles in the left hand (either will do), lift the first stitch over the second, as for the basic cast-/bind-off. Repeat both steps until all the stitches have been cast/bound off.

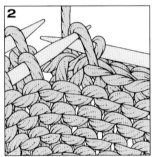

The double cast-/bind-off is a good way to bind off two pieces of knitting at the same time, whilst creating a neat, sturdy seam between them.

Invisible cast-/bind-off

This ingenious method of casting/binding off a single rib fabric may seem complex at first, but the results are worth the effort. It makes a highly professional finish on a ribbed collar or neckband.

To practise, cast on an odd number of stitches – at least 25 – and work in K1, P1 rib for about 4cm (1½in), ending with a wrong-side row. Cut off the thread, allowing 3 times the width of the knitting, and thread the end into a tapestry needle. In the illustrations this is shown in a contrasting colour for clarity. The knit stitches have odd numbers, the purl stitches have even ones.

You work into each stitch twice; the first time in the opposite direction to its construction, the second time in the same direction. Only then do you slip the stitch slipped off the needle.

1 To begin, insert the blunt-ended yarn needle purlwise into stitch 1, then knitwise into stitch 2. Leave these stitches on the needle. Work knitwise into stitch 1 and slip it off the needle.

2 Work purlwise into stitch 3. Work purlwise into stitch 2 and slip it off the needle.

Take the yarn needle behind stitch 3 and to the front between stitches 3 and 4. Work knitwise into stitch 4. Repeat steps 2–5, working into stitches 3, 5, 4 and 6 . Continue in this way to the end of the row.

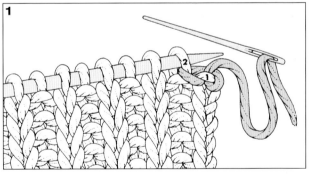

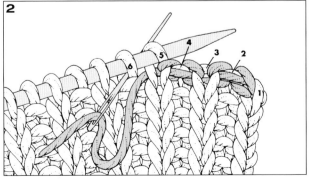

Grafting

Grafting is a method of sewing two knitted edges together stitch by stitch, so that the seam is invisible. The sewing stitches duplicate the structure of the knitting. This technique is often used to join a front and back section at the shoulder. The edges need not be straight, as shown; they could be shaped, as shown on page 82. To work the grafting, you can either place the pieces on a flat surface, as shown in these illustrations, or hold them together with wrong sides facing and the needles close together in your hand. Grafting can also be used to join an edge that has been cast on using the invisible Method 2 (see page 81).

Grafting garter stitch

Although most often used on stocking/stockinette stitch, grafting can be used on other patterns, such as garter stitch.

End one piece on a right-side row, the other on a wrong-side row, so that the lower piece will have a ridge close to the needle and the other piece will have the ridge one row away.

1 Take the needle purlwise through the first stitch on the lower edge, purlwise through the first upper stitch and then knitwise through the next upper stitch.

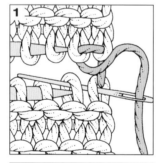

2 *Insert the needle knitwise again through the first lower stitch, then purlwise through the second lower stitch.

3 Insert the needle purlwise through the upper stitch, then knitwise through the next upper stitch. Repeat from * to end.

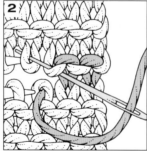

Grafting stocking/stockinette stitch

1 End one piece of knitting with a knit row and the other with a purl row, so that when the work is positioned as shown the needles will both point to the right.

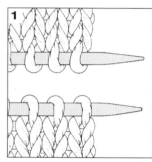

2 Thread a yarn needle with matching yarn, 3 times the width of the knitted edge. Insert the needle purlwise through the first stitch on the lower edge, then purlwise through the opposite stitch on the upper edge. Take it knitwise through the first stitch again, then purlwise through the second stitch on the same edge.

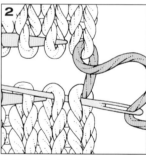

3 *Insert the needle knitwise into the stitch on the upper edge where the yarn emerges, then purlwise into the next stitch to the left. Insert it knitwise into the stitch just below, then purlwise into the next stitch to the left. Repeat from * to end.

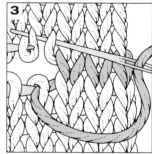

Hems, facings and waistbands

Hems are needed wherever a reasonably firm edge that lies flat is required: on the lower and front opening edges of a tailored jacket, for example. A vertical hem is normally called a facing. It is sometimes possible – when working a skirt, for example – to work from the top downwards, ending with the hem. The hem edge stitches can be cast/bound off, or left on the needle and sewn to the main fabric using the stitch-by-stitch method (see page 86). A knitted waistband is similar to a hem. This is often worked in single ribbing and used on garments for babies or young children, as the extra-snug fit compensates for the lack of a natural waistline. You can produce a less bulky alternative to a knitted waistband by working it in herringbone stitch.

Sewn-in hem with ridge foldline

This hem is best suited to a garment worked in stocking/stockinette stitch. Use a cast-on method with a fairly flat edge.

If you plan to use the stitch-by-stitch sewing method (see page 86) for attaching the hem, use the invisible cast-on Method 2 (see page 81). For the hem itself, use needles one or two sizes smaller than those specified for the main fabric. This helps it to lie smoothly when turned up.

1 Work in stocking/stockinette stitch for the required depth of the hem, ending with a wrong-side row.

2 On the next (right-side) row, purl, rather than knit, to produce a ridge on the fabric. This will serve as the foldline on the hem.

3 Change to larger needles and continue in stocking/stockinette stitch for the main part of the garment.

Sewn-in hem with slipstitch foldline

This hem is more suitable for garments worked in textured stitch patterns or heavyweight yarn.

1 Work the depth of the hem in stocking/stockinette stitch, using smaller needles, as for the ridge foldline hem, ending with a wrong-side row.

2 On the next (right-side) row, work as follows: *K1, wyf sl 1, rep from * to last st, K1.

3 Change to larger needles and work the main part of the garment in pattern.

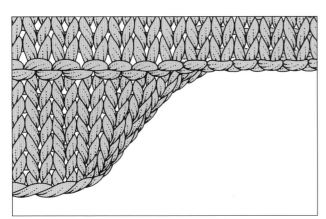

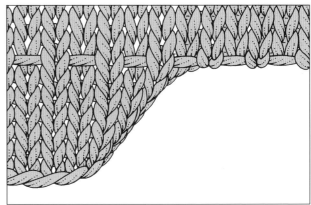

Sewn-in hem with picot foldline

This hem is best worked in a fine yarn.

1 Cast on an odd number of stitches, and work in stocking/stockinette stitch, using smaller needles, to the desired depth, ending with a wrong-side row.

2 On the next (right-side) row, work as follows: *K2tog, yf, rep from * to last st, K1.

3 Change to larger needles, and continue in pattern. When completed, turn up the hem along the line of eyelets to produce the picot effect.

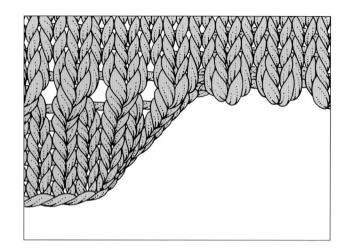

Whipstitch

This stitch is suitable for sewing up the hem on a garment worked in a light- or medium-weight yarn. Work through a single purled loop of the main fabric, then through a loop on the hem edge as shown.

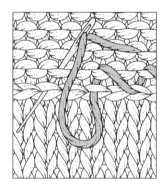

Blind hemming stitch

This method is suitable for a heavyweight fabric. You may need to separate the yarn and use one or two plies to reduce bulk. First tack the hem in place, about 1cm (⅜in) below the edge. Turn the garment as shown, with the hem fold away from you. Work the stitches between the hem edge and the main fabric so that the hem edge is free.

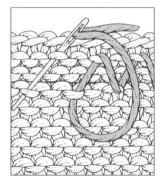

Stitch-by-stitch method

You can use this method on an edge that has been cast on using the invisible Method 2 or on the edge of a section that has been worked from the top down. In the first case, remove the foundation yarn gradually as you work the hem; in the second, leave the needle in the work, removing it as you stitch.

1 Secure the sewing yarn at the RH edge, and insert the needle purlwise through the first stitch on the lower edge. Take it through the corresponding stitch in the main fabric, then knitwise through the first lower stitch. Insert the needle knitwise through the next stitch on the lower edge, then purlwise into the next stitch above.

2 Continue working in this way to the end.

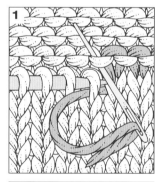

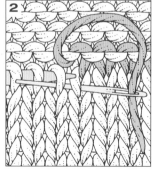

Knitted-in hem

This is an ingenious way of turning up a hem, but you must work it carefully if it is not to look bulky. Before knitting the garment itself, work a small sample and adjust the hem needle size and the number of rows if necessary. The needles you use for the hem should be two or three sizes smaller than those used for the main fabric.

1 Cast on the required number of stitches and work the hem allowance as for a sewn-in hem. Work a ridge or slipstitch foldline, and continue with the larger needles until the main part of the garment is the same depth as the hem allowance, ending with a wrong-side row. Leave the stitches on the needle.

2 Using a spare needle and working on the right side, pick up and knit stitches along the cast-on edge. Work into the farthest loop of each stitch – the one that is closer to the garment. Fasten off the extra yarn.

3 Turn up the hem along the ridge. Using the main yarn and working on the right side of the garment, knit one stitch from the garment with one stitch from the hem all along the row. The picked-up stitches from the hem are now securely knitted into the main fabric.

Mitred hem and facing

For a neat finish on the lower edges of a jacket, work a hem and facing with a mitred corner. First calculate, from the garment tension/gauge, the number of stitches to cast on for the hem. Find the number of stitches in 2.5cm (1in), and subtract this from the number required for the full width of the section.

1 Cast on the reduced number of stitches and work in stocking/stockinette stitch, increasing 1 stitch at the front edge on every alternate row until you have the total number are on the needle.

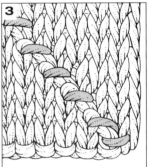

2 Work the turning ridge, then continue increasing, working a slipstitch foldline (above). When the facing is the same depth as the hem, work straight to continue.

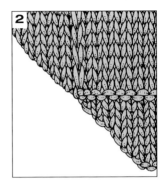

3 When complete, overcast stitch the diagonal edges neatly together.

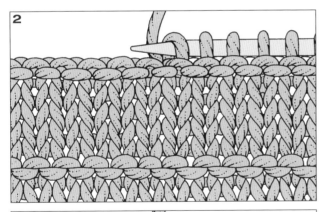

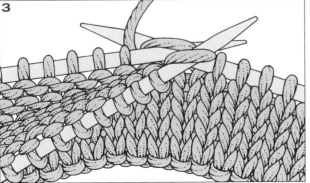

Vertical facing

A vertical facing may be required on the front edge of a jacket, for example, and should always be worked in stocking/stockinette stitch. The illustration shows a left front edge; reverse the process for a right front edge.

On a right-side row, work in pattern to the foldline; slip the next stitch purlwise; continue in stocking/stockinette stitch to the end of the row. On a wrong-side row, work in stocking/stockinette stitch up to and including the slipped stitch; continue in pattern to the end. When the section is complete, turn the facing to the wrong side along the foldline and sew it in place using whipstitch: work from right to left, taking the needle alternately through one stitch of the main fabric and then through the corresponding stitch on the edge of the facing.

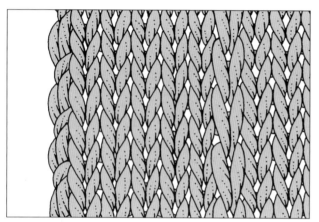

Herringbone casing

1 Sew the ends of the elastic together to form a ring, first making sure that it fits the waist smoothly without stretching. Divide the elastic into 4 equal sections and mark them with pins. Mark the skirt edge into quarters.

2 Pin the elastic to the wrong side of the waist edge, matching the points on the skirt edge.

3 Secure the knitting yarn to the fabric with two backstitches, just below the elastic. Take it up over the elastic and to the right, and insert the needle through the edge of the knitting from right to left. Take it down to the right and insert it again from the left. Continue around the waistband; secure firmly.

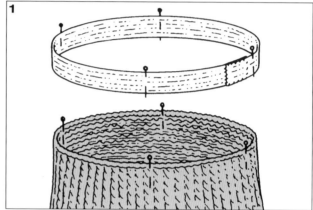

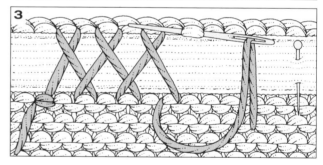

Knitted waistband

1 Work a ridge foldline as shown on page 85, then knit the waistband in Kl, Pl rib until you have reached the required depth.

2 Sew the waistband in place, leaving about 5cm (2in) unstitched.

3 Thread elastic through the casing, and pin the ends together with a safety pin. Check the fit. Sew the ends together firmly, then complete the stitching on the casing edge to finish.

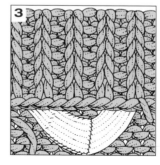

Pockets

The three most popular styles of pocket are the patch pocket, the horizontal inside pocket and the vertical inside pocket. There are various methods of working them; you can often substitute a method you prefer for the one in a pattern. Patch pockets are usually most successful in a textured stitch pattern, which provides contrast. A stocking/stockinette stitch patch pocket can have a homemade look if it is not sewn on carefully. If a stocking/stockinette stitch pocket is required, a neat way of attaching it is with Swiss darning. Alternatively, work a modified patch pocket on stitches picked up from the main fabric. Working a garter stitch selvedge along the two sides will provide a neat finish. You can attach a patch pocket leaving one of the side edges unstitched, instead of the top edge, to make a vertical patch pocket.

Embroidering on a patch pocket

1 Work the patch to the desired size and cast/bind off. Block or press it as appropriate, and darn in the ends. Pin the pocket to the garment. Secure the yarn (shown here in a contrasting colour for clarity) to the lower RH corner on the wrong side of the main fabric, and bring it up in the centre of the first stitch in from the edge as shown.

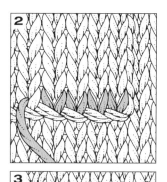

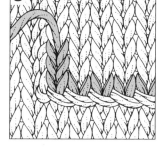

2 Work Swiss darning (see page 70) over all the stitches across the lower edge of the pocket.

3 Continue up the LH side of the pocket as shown. Sew on the RH edge of the pocket in the same way.

Patch pocket on picked-up stitches

This style of pocket, too, is worked after the main section has been completed.

1 Secure the yarn to the wrong side of the work at the position of the lower RH corner of the pocket. Using a crochet hook, pick up the required number of stitches for the pocket and place them on the needle.

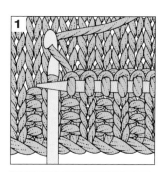

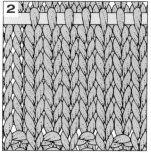

2 Beginning with a purl row, work in stocking/stockinette stitch to the required depth for the pocket. Cast/bind off evenly.

3 Sew the side edges of the pocket in place, either with Swiss darning or with overcast stitches.

Oversewing a patch pocket

1 Lay the pocket on the main section, and insert a pin diagonally at each corner, pinning through the background fabric only. Remove the pocket, and check that the pins are aligned on the same vertical and horizontal rows.

2 Take two fine double-pointed needles and insert them in the fabric between the pins, picking up alternate stitches.

3 Place the pocket between the needles, and oversew it to the picked-up stitches, working into the alternating stitches along the pocket edge. When both sides have been sewn, oversew the lower edge in place, again working through alternate stitches.

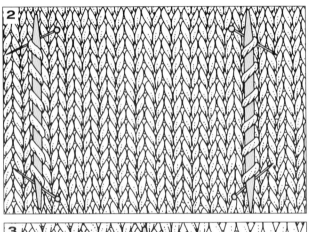

Horizontal inside pocket

A pattern will often instruct you to place a horizontal pocket by leaving the stitches for the border on a spare needle, joining in the pocket lining and then picking up the opening stitches and working the border. The following method incorporates the border stitches in the fabric, producing a slightly neater finish.

1 First work the pocket lining, casting on 2 more stitches than are allowed for the opening. Work the lining to the required depth, ending with a knit row and decreasing 1 stitch at each end of the previous purl row. Leave the stitches on a spare needle.

2 Work the main fabric up to the position for the pocket border. Continue knitting, working the border in the chosen pattern. When the border is the required depth, cast/bind off these stitches on a right-side row; work to the end.

3 On the next row, purl across to the beginning of the pocket opening, then purl across the stitches of the pocket lining and continue to the end of the row.

4 When the section is complete, oversew the pocket lining edges in place on the wrong side.

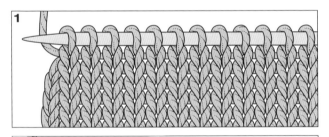

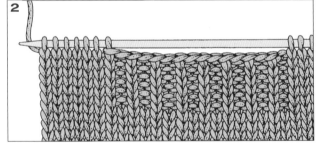

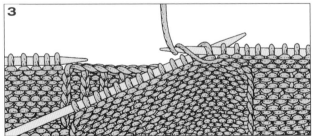

Vertical pockets with borders included

You work the opening for a vertical pocket in two stages, first one side and then the other. When the second side is as deep as the first, you rejoin the two sides. You can then incorporate a pocket lining in the outer side section of the fabric. You can either knit the border of a vertical pocket along with the top part of the pocket or work it later on picked-up stitches. The illustrations show a pocket in the right side of a garment. For the left side, reverse the instructions.

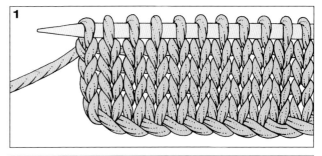

1 Work a few rows of stocking/stockinette stitch for the lower part of the pocket lining. End with a right-side row, and place the stitches on a spare needle.

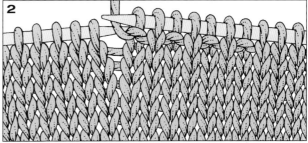

2 Work the main section up to the level for the pocket opening, ending with a wrong-side row. On the next row, work across to the inner edge of the border, then work in the border pattern across the specified number of stitches. Slip the remaining stitches for the outer side section on to a spare needle.

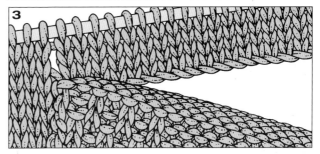

3 Continue working on the top section of the pocket until it is the required depth, ending with a right-side row. Slip these stitches on to a spare needle; do not break off the yarn. Now pick up the pocket lining; place it alongside the outer side section, join on new yarn if necessary, and knit to the end of the row.

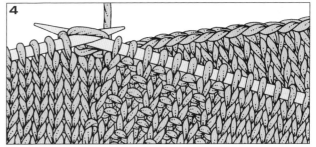

4 Continue working across the outer side section and pocket lining until this piece is one row shorter than the top section, ending with a wrong-side row. On the next row, cast/bind off the pocket lining stitches. Rejoin the two sections of the main fabric; knit to the end of the row. Sew the pocket lining to the main fabric using whipstitch.

Pocket with border added

Work this pocket as for the one with a knitted border, but do not work the border stitches. (The division should be placed slightly closer to the centre front.) When the section is completed, pick up stitches along the edge of the top section of the pocket and work in the chosen pattern. Sew the edges to the main fabric.

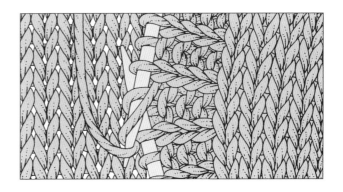

Fastenings

Fastenings can be problematical in a knitted garment because the fabric is soft and stretchy and is inclined to pull away from a zip or buttons. When inserting a zip, it is important to provide a firm edge for the zip opening. If the knitting is in a heavyweight yarn, this is best done by working a selvedge; on lightweight knitting, use crochet.

Inserting a zip – selvedge opening

When working the garment, add 2 stitches to the opening edges, and work a double garter stitch selvedge (see page 27). Block or press the completed sections.

1 Place the adjacent sections right side up, and tack them together using an overcasting stitches and a blunt-ended yarn needle.

2 Turn the work wrong side up. Open the zip and place it over the opening with the teeth exactly centred. Using an ordinary sewing needle, tack the zip tape to the knitting down one side. Close the zip; continue tacking up the other side.

3 Working from the right side and using strong sewing thread such as buttonhole twist, sew the zip in place with backstitch. Start at the top and work down one side and up the other.

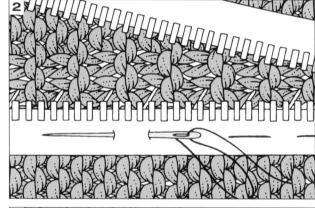

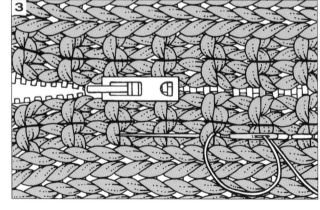

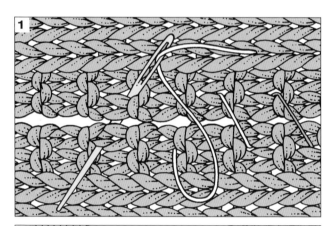

Crocheted zip opening

1 Before sewing in the zip, work a row of double crochet (see page 77) along the opening edges.

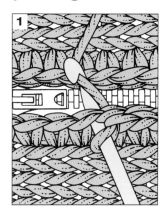

2 Tack and stitch the zip in place as described for a selvedge opening (see opposite), working the backstitch along the outer edge of the crochet.

3 Open the zip and work crochet slip stitches (see page 77) into the double crochet stitches.

Ribbon-faced buttonhole band

To prevent the button and buttonhole bands of a cardigan from sagging, sew a length of ribbon (grosgrain is the usual choice, but any firm ribbon will do) to the underside of the bands.

1 Cut the ribbon about 3cm (1¼in) longer than the band. Turn under one end and tack it to the knitting; trim the other end if necessary, and turn it under. Slipstitch the ribbon in place as shown.

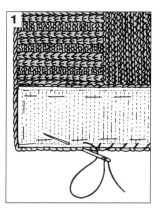

2 To finish, turn the buttonhole band right side up and cut a slit in the ribbon under each buttonhole, taking care not to cut into the knitting. Using yarn or matching perlé cotton and a chenille needle (a large-eyed sharp-pointed embroidery needle), work buttonhole stitch around the buttonholes.

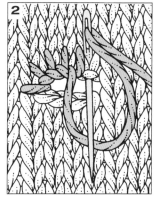

This zip has been worked into the firm cast-/bound-off edge of the cushion (see pages 152–155) so there is no need for a selvedge.

There is no greater joy than receiving a hand-knitted gift for a new baby. Mums and dads delight in cute knitted hats and bootees, and really appreciate the personal element they contribute to the occasion; hand-knitted baby items are often treasured for years to come. You can choose from a handful of lovely projects: a blanket for a newborn, tiny baby slippers, a snuggle cardigan and a cosy hat and mittens. All of the projects are either easy or intermediate skill level and can be adapted for boys or girls simply by changing the colourways.

Beautiful for babies

Baby blanket

This stripy blanket is fun to knit – and relatively quick to make, as finishing is minimal. With its fresh colour scheme, it will give a touch of class to the nursery.

Skill level
Intermediate

Techniques
- Yarn-forward increase (page 30)
- Knitting two stitches together (page 31)
- Slipped stitch decrease (page 32)
- Intarsia (pages 62–63)
- Darning in ends (page 37)

Tools
1 pair of 5mm (UK 6) (US 8) knitting needles
Basic equipment for finishing (see page 35)

Materials
Rowan All Seasons Cotton
3 × 50g (1¾oz) balls in Bleached, 182 (**A**)

3 × balls in Lime Leaf, 217 (**B**)

3 × balls in Ravish, 199 (**C**)

Tension/gauge
17 sts and 24 rows to 10cm/4in measured over st st on 5mm (UK 6) (US 8) needles. Change needle size if necessary to obtain correct tension/gauge.

Abbreviations
See page 6.

Note
When changing colour always twist the yarns on the WS of your work, as explained for the intarsia technique (see pages 62–63), to avoid leaving a hole.

Measurements
Finished size
88 × 68cm (34½ × 26¾in)

(2) 2 to go!

Blanket

Using yarn A cast on 25 sts, using B cast on 25 sts, using C cast on 25 sts, using A cast on 25 sts, using B cast on 25 sts, using C cast on 25 sts. 150 sts.

Keeping each colour correct and twisting yarns at back of work cont as follows:

Row 1 K.

Row 2 P.

Now work in diamond patt as follows:

Row 1 *K11, yf, sl 1, K2tog, psso, yf, K11, rep from * All stitches to end.

Row 2 and every foll alternate row P. ✓

Row 3 *K10, K2tog, yf, k1, yf, sl 1, K1, psso, K10, rep All stitches from * to end.

Row 5 *K9, K2tog, yf, K3, yf, sl 1, psso, K9, rep from * to end. 1 stitch over.

Row 7 *K8, K2tog, yf, K5, yf, sl 1, K1, psso, K8, rep from * to end. K7

Row 9 *K7, K2tog, yf, K7, yf, sl 1, K1, psso, K7, rep from * to end. K6.

Row 11 *K6, K2tog, yf, K9, yf, sl 1, K1, psso, K6, rep from * to end.

Row 13 *K5, K2tog, yf, K11, yf, sl 1, K1, psso, K5, rep from * to end.

Row 15 *K4, K2tog, yf, K13, yf, sl 1, K1, psso, K4, rep from * to end.

Row 17 *K3, K2tog, yf, K15, yf, sl 1, K1, psso, K3, rep from * to end.

Row 19 *K2, K2tog, yf, K17, yf, sl 1, K1, psso, K2, rep from * to end.

Row 21 *K1, K2tog, yf, K19, yf, sl 1, K1, psso, K1, rep from * to end.

Row 23 *K2, yf, sl 1, K1, psso, K17, K2tog, yf, K2, rep from * to end.

Row 25 *K3, yf, sl 1, K1, psso, K15, K2tog, yf, K3, rep from * to end.

Row 27 *K4, yf, sl 1, K1, psso, K13, K2tog, yf, K4, rep from * to end.

Row 29 *K5, yf, sl 1, K1, psso, K11, K2tog, yf, K5, rep from * to end.

Row 31 *K6, yf, sl 1, K1, psso, K9, K2tog, yf, K6, rep from * to end.

Row 33 *K7, yf, sl 1, K1, psso, K7, K2tog, yf, K7, rep from * to end.

Row 35 *K8, yf, sl 1, K1, psso, K5, K2tog, yf, K8, rep from * to end.

Row 37 *K9, yf, sl 1, K1, psso, K3, K2tog, yf, K9, rep from * to end

Row 39 *K10, yf, sl 1, K1, psso, K1, K2tog, yf, K10, rep from * to end.

Row 40 P.

These 40 rows form diamond patt. Cont in diamond patt. Rep rows 1–40 three more times, then work rows 1 and 2 again. Cast/bind off in each colour.

Next Row K.

Next Row P.

To finish

Darn in loose ends. Press carefully, following instructions on yarn label and using a pressing cloth.

Baby slippers

These adorable little slippers make a charming gift for a new baby and will be treasured in years to come as a reminder of tiny infant feet.

Skill level
Intermediate

Techniques
- Garter stitch (page 19)
- Bar increase (page 28)
- Knitting or purling two stitches together (page 31)
- Multiple increase (page 81)
- Darning in ends (page 37)
- Seams (page 36)

Tools
1 pair of 4mm (UK 8) (US 6) knitting needles
Basic equipment for finishing (see page 35)

Materials
Rowan Kid Classic
1 × 50g (1¾oz) ball in Glacier, 822
or
Feather, 828

60cm/24in of coordinating organza ribbon

Tension/gauge
22 sts and 40 rows to 10cm/4in measured over garter st using 4mm (UK 8) (US 6) needles. Change needle size if necessary to obtain correct tension/gauge.

Abbreviations
See page 6.

Measurements

Size
To fit	0–3 months	3–6 months	6–9 months

Actual measurements
Length of foot	9cm (3½in)	10cm (4in)	11cm (4½in)

Slippers

Cast on 14 (14:16) sts.

Working in garter st throughout, cont as follows:

Inc 1 st at each end of next and foll 2 (3:3) alt rows.
20 (22:24] sts.

Work 3 (1:3) rows.

Dec 1 st at each end of next and foll 2 (3:3) alt rows,
ending with WS facing for next row. 14 (14:16) sts.
This completes sole section.

Shape heel

Cast on 4 (5:6) sts at beg of next row. 18 (19:22) sts.

Inc 1 st at beg of next and foll 2 (3:3) alt rows, ending
with WS facing for next row. 21 (23:26) sts.

Shape foot opening

Cast/bind off 12 (13:15) sts at beg of next row (for
foot opening). 9 (10:11) sts.

Work 9 (11:15) rows, ending with WS facing for
next row.

Shape second side of heel

Cast on 12 (13:15) sts at beg of next row (for other
side of foot opening). 21 (23:26) sts.

Dec 1 st at beg of next and foll 2 (3:3) alt rows.

Cast/bind off rem 18 (19:22) sts.

To finish

Do NOT press.

Darn in ends. Sew together row-end edges of heel
sections. Easing in fullness, sew upper section to sole
along heel, toe and side edges. Cut ribbon into 2 equal
lengths and sew to sides of foot opening as shown in
photograph. Tie ends in a bow on top of foot.

Snuggle cardigan

A versatile extra layer that will look and feel great over a simple one-piece garment or a party dress.

Skill level
Intermediate

Techniques
- Bar increases (page 28)
- Knitting or purling two stitches together (page 31)
- Multiple increase (page 81)
- Pressing (page 35)
- Seams (page 36)
- Picking up stitches (page 33)
- Eyelet buttonhole (page 34)
- Darning in ends (page 37)

Tools
1 pair of 3.25mm (UK 10) (US 3) knitting needles
1 pair of 4mm (UK 8) (US 6) knitting needles

2 stitch markers
1 stitch holder
Basic equipment for finishing (see page 35)

Materials
Rowan Wool Cotton
3 × (3:4:5) 50g (1¾oz) balls in Clear, 941 **(A)**

1 × ball in Antique, 900 **(B)**

Alternative colours
Variation 1
Antique, 900 **(A)**

Bilberry Fool, 959 **(B)**

Variation 2
Citron, 901 **(A)**

Elf, 946 **(B)**

5 buttons

Tension/gauge
23 sts and 32 rows to 10cm/4in measured over pattern using 4mm (UK 8) (US 6) needles. Change needle size if necessary to obtain correct tension/gauge.

Abbreviations
See page 6.

Measurements

Size	1	2	3	4
To fit	0–3 months	3–6 months	6–12 months	12–18 months
Chest	41cm (16in)	46cm (18in)	51cm (20in)	56cm (22in)
Actual measurements				
Chest	46cm (18in)	51cm (20in)	57cm (22½in)	62cm (24½in)
Length	21cm (8¼in)	25cm (9¾in)	29cm (11½in)	33cm (13in)
Sleeve seam	12cm (4¾in)	15cm (6in)	19cm (7½in)	22cm (8½in)

Body

The Body is worked in one piece, starting at back cast-on edge.

Using smaller needles and yarn B, cast on 53 (59: 65:71) sts.

Rows 1–3 Using B, K.

Join in A.

Rows 4 and 5 Using A, K.

Rows 6 and 7 Using B, K.

Break off B and cont using A only.

Change to larger needles.

Now work in patt as follows:

Row 1 (RS) K.

Row 2 P.

Row 3 K1, *P1, K1, rep from * to end.

Row 4 P.

These 4 rows form patt.

Cont in patt until Back measures 6 (9:12:15)cm/2¼(3½: 4¾:6)in, ending with RS facing for next row.

Shape for sleeves

Inc 1 st at each end of next and 2 foll 4th rows, then on foll 2 alt rows, then on foll 3 rows, taking inc sts into patt and ending with RS facing for next row. 69 (75: 81:87) sts.

Cast on 15 (22:31:39) sts at beg of next 2 rows. 99 (119: 143:165) sts.

Cont straight until work measures 10 (11:12:13)cm/ 4 (4¼:4¾:5)in from sleeve cast-on sts, ending with RS facing for next row.

Divide for fronts

Place a marker at both ends of last row to denote shoulder/overarm 'seam'.

Next row (RS) Patt 39 (48:59:69) sts and slip these sts on to a holder for Right Front, cast/bind off next 21 (23:25:27) sts (for back neck), patt to end.

Work on this last set of 39 (48:59:69) sts only for Left Front.

Work 3 rows, ending with RS facing for next row.

Inc 1 st at neck edge of next and foll 2 alt rows, then on foll 3 rows, taking inc sts into patt and ending with RS facing for next row. 45 (54:65:75) sts.

Cast on 3 (4:5:6) sts at beg of next row. 48 (58: 70:81) sts.

Cont straight until work measures 10 (11:12:13)cm/ 4 (4¼:4¾:5)in from marker, ending with WS facing for next row.

Shape for sleeve

Keeping patt correct, cast/bind off 15 (22:31:39) sts at beg of next row. 33 (36:39:42) sts.

Work 1 row.

Dec 1 st at sleeve edge on next 4 rows, then on foll 2 alt rows, then on 2 foll 4th rows. 25 (28:31:34) sts.

Work straight until work measures 4 (7:10:13)cm/ 1½ (2¾:4:5)in from sleeve cast-off/bound-off sts, ending with RS facing for next row.

Change to smaller needles.

Join in B.

Using B, K 2 rows.

Using A, K 2 rows.

Using B, K 3 rows, ending with WS facing for next row. Cast/bind off knitwise (on WS).

Return to sts left on holder, rejoin yarn with WS facing and patt to end. Complete Right Front to match Left Front, reversing shapings.

To finish

Press carefully following instructions on yarn label.

Neckband

With RS facing, using smaller needles and B, and starting and ending at top of front opening edges, pick up and K 15 (16:17:18) sts up right side of front neck, 21 (23:25:27) sts from back neck cast-off/bound-off edge, then 15 (16:17:18) sts down left side of front neck. 51 (55:59:63) sts.

**Row 1 (WS) Using B, K.

Join in A.

Rows 2 and 3 Using A, K.

Rows 4–6 Using B, K.

Using B, cast/bind off knitwise (on WS). ******

Button band

With RS facing, using smaller needles and B, pick up and K 43 (51:63:71) sts evenly along one front opening edge (Left Front for a girl, Right Front for a boy), between top of neckband and front cast-off/bound-off edge.

Work as given for Neckband from ** to **.

Buttonhole band

Work as given for Button Band, picking up sts along other front opening edge but adding 5 buttonholes in row 2 as follows:

Row 2 (RS) K2, *K2tog, yf (to make a buttonhole), K7 (9:12:14), rep from * 3 more times, K2tog, yf (to make 5th buttonhole), K3.

Cuffs (make 2 alike)

With RS facing, using smaller needles and B, pick up and K 39 (43:47:51) sts evenly along row-end edge of sleeve section.

Work as given for Neckband from ** to **.

Sew side and sleeve seams. Darn in loose ends. Sew on buttons.

Baby's hat and mittens

Perfect for chilly days outside, this hat and mitten set will feel wonderfully soft on a baby's delicate skin.

Skill level
Easy

Techniques
- Knitting two stitches together (page 31)
- Horizontal stripes (page 60)
- Darning in ends (page 37)
- Pressing (page 35)
- Seams (page 36)

Tools
1 pair of 2.75mm (UK 12) (US 2) knitting needles
1 pair of 3.25mm (UK 10) (US 3) knitting needles
Basic equipment for finishing (see page 35)

Materials
Rowan 4-ply Soft
1 × ball in Whisper, 395 **(A)**

1 × 50g (1¾oz) ball in Nippy, 376 **(B)**

Alternative colours
Variation 1
Fairy, 370**(A)**

Nippy, 376 **(B)**

Variation 2
Irish Cream, 386 **(A)**

Nippy, 376 **(B)**

Tension/gauge
28 sts and 36 rows to 10cm/4in measured over pattern using 3.25mm (UK 10) (US 3) needles. Change needle size if necessary to obtain correct tension/gauge.

Abbreviations
See page 6.

Measurements – Hat

Size	1	2	3	4
To fit	0–3 months	3–6 months	6–12 months	12–18 months
Width around head	35cm (13¾in)	37cm (14½in)	39cm (15¼in)	41cm (16in)

Measurements – Mittens

Size	1	2	3
Finished size	13 × 8.5cm (5 × 3¼in)	16 × 9.5cm (6¼ × 3¾in)	19 × 10.5cm (7½ × 4in)

Hat

Using larger needles and yarn A, cast on 97 (103: 109:115) sts.

Row 1 (RS) K1, *P1, K1, rep from * to end.
Row 2 P1, *K1, P1, rep from * to end.
These 2 rows form rib patt.
Join in B.
Using B, work in rib for 2 rows.
Using A, work in rib for 2 rows.
Rep last 4 rows until Hat measures 8cm/3in, ending after 2 rows using B.
Break off B and cont using A only.
Now work in patt as follows:
Row 1 (RS) K.
Row 2 and every foll alt row P.
Row 3 K3, P1, *K5, P1, rep from * to last 3 sts, K3.
Row 5 K.
Row 7 P1, *K5, P1, rep from * to end.
Row 8 P.
These 8 rows form patt.
Cont in patt until Hat measures 15 (16:17:18)cm/ 6 (6¼:6½:7)in, ending with RS facing for next row.
Shape crown
Row 1 (RS) *K4, K2tog, rep from * to last st, K1. 81 (86:91:96) sts.
Row 2 P.
Row 3 K.
Row 4 P.
Row 5 *K3, K2tog, rep from * to last st, K1. 65 (69: 73:77) sts.
Rows 6–8 As rows 2–4.
Row 9 *K2, K2tog, rep from * to last st, K1. 49 (52: 55:58) sts.
Row 10 P.
Row 11 *K1, K2tog, rep from * to last st, K1. 33 (35: 37:39) sts.
Row 12 P.
Row 13 *K2tog, rep from * to last st, K1. 17 (18: 19:20) sts.
Row 14 P1 (0:1:0), (P2tog) 8 (9:9:10) times.
Break yarn and thread through rem 9 (9:10:10) sts. Pull up tight and fasten off securely.

To finish hat

Press carefully, following instructions on yarn label.
Darn in loose ends.
Sew back seam, reversing seam for first 6cm/2¼in for turn-back. Fold 4cm/1½in turn-back to outside.

Mittens (make 4)

Using smaller needles and yarn B, cast on 19 (23: 27) sts.
Row 1 K1, *P1, K1, rep from * to end.
Row 2 P1, *K1, P1, rep from * to end.
These 2 rows form rib.
Join in A.
Using A, work in rib for 2 rows.
Using B, work in rib for 2 rows.
Rep last 4 rows once more.
Change to larger needles and A.
Now work in patt as follows:
Row 1 (RS) K.
Row 2 and every foll alt row P.
Row 3 K3 (5:7), P1, K5, P1, K5, P1, K3 (5:7).
Row 5 K.
Row 7 K0 (2:4), P1, K5, P1, K5, P1, K5, P1, K0 (2:4).
Row 8 P.
These 8 rows form patt. Cont in patt until mitten measures 7 (8:9)cm/2¾ (3:3½)in.
Keeping patt correct, dec 1 st at each end of next and foll 5 rows.
Cast/bind off rem 7 (11:15) sts.

To finish mittens

Darn in loose ends. Block the pieces. Place 2 mitten pieces together with right sides facing and sew together along both side edges and across top edges using backstitch or an edge-to-edge seam.

Children always look adorable in hand-knitted clothes and here are four great projects for toddlers and young children from one to six years old. Knit a rugged hoodie in bold stripes for an adventurous boy's outdoor exploits, or opt for the cosy, cutesy heart-patterned jumper for a girl who loves pink. For keeping snug outside, no trend-setting toddler should be without the fabulous tassel hat, and if you feel ready for a challenge, the scarf and mittens combo is worth the extra effort.

Cute for kids

Rugged hoodie

A cotton cover-up perfect for chilly days, this will make a great addition to any discerning young child's wardrobe!

Skill level
Intermediate

Techniques
- Stocking/stockinette stitch (page 19)
- Bar increases (page 28)
- Knitting or purling two stitches together (page 31)
- Horizontal stripes (page 60)
- Purling stitches together 'tbl' (page 31)
- Picking up stitches (page 33)
- Eyelet buttonholes (page 34)
- Pressing (page 35)
- Seams (page 36)

Tools
1 pair of 3.25mm (UK 10) (US 3) knitting needles
1 pair of 4mm (UK 8) (US 6) knitting needles
3.25mm (UK 10) (US 3) circular knitting needle
3 stitch holders
1 stitch marker
Basic equipment for finishing (see page 35)

Materials
Rowan Handknit Cotton
5 × (5:6:6) 50g (1¾oz) balls in Bleached, 263 (**A**)

1 × ball in Bermuda, 324 (**B**)

1 × ball in Celery, 309 (**C**)

1 × ball in Turkish Plum, 277 (**D**)

Alternative colours
Variation 1
Bleached, 263 (**A**)

Slick, 313 (**B**)

Sugar, 303 (**C**)

Rose, 332 (**D**)

Variation 2
Linen, 205 (**A**)

Ice Water, 239 (**B**)

Raffia, 330 (**C**)

Slippery, 316 (**D**)

5 buttons

Tension/gauge
20 sts and 28 rows to 10cm/4in measured over st st using 4mm (UK 8) (US 6) needles. Change needle size if necessary to obtain correct tension/gauge.

Abbreviations
See page 6.

Notes
When working striped pattern, carry A loosely up the side of the work.

Measurements

Size	1	2	3	4
To fit	1–2 years	2–3 years	3–4 years	4–5 years
Chest	46cm (18in)	51cm (20in)	56cm (22in)	61cm (24in)
Actual measurements				
Chest	58cm (22¾in)	64cm (25¼in)	70cm (27½in)	76cm (30in)
Length	27cm (10½in)	31cm (12¼in)	35cm (13¾in)	40cm (15¾in)
Sleeve seam	16cm (6¼in)	20cm (7¾in)	26cm (10¼in)	30cm (11¾in)

Back

Using smaller pair of needles and yarn A, cast on
58 (62:70:74) sts.
Row 1 (RS) K2, *P2, K2, rep from * to end.
Row 2 P2, *K2, P2, rep from * to end.
These 2 rows form rib patt.
Work in rib patt for 6 more rows, inc 0 (1:0:1) st at each
end of last row and ending with RS facing for next row.
58 (64:70:76) sts.
Change to larger needles.
Starting with a K row and joining in colours as required,
work in striped st st patt as follows:
Rows 1 and 2 Using A.
Rows 3–6 Using B.
Rows 7 and 8 Using A.
Rows 9–12 Using C.
Rows 13 and 14 Using A.
Rows 15–18 Using D.
These 18 rows form striped st st patt.
Cont in patt until Back measures 14 (17:20:24)cm/5½
(6½:73/4:9½)in, ending with RS facing for next row.

Shape armholes
Keeping stripes correct, cast/bind off 3 sts at beg of
next 2 rows. 52 (58:64:70) sts.
Dec 1 st at each end of next and foll 3 alt rows. 44 (50:
56:62) sts.
Work straight until armhole measures approx 13 (14:
15:16)cm/5 (5½:6:6¼.7)in, ending after 2 rows using A
and with RS facing for next row.
Break off B, C and D and cont using A only.

Shape shoulders
Cast/bind off 4 (5:5:6) sts at beg of next 4 rows, then
4 (4:6:6) sts at beg of foll 2 rows.
Break yarn and leave rem 20 (22:24:26) sts on a holder.

Left front

Using smaller pair of needles and A, cast on 27 (31:
31:35) sts.
Row 1 (RS) K2, *P2, K2, rep from * to last st, K1.
Row 2 K1, P2, *K2, P2, rep from * to end.
These 2 rows form rib patt.
Work in rib patt for 6 more rows, dec (dec:inc:inc)
0 (1:2:1) sts evenly across last row and ending with
RS facing for next row. 27 (30:33:36) sts.
Change to larger needles.
Starting with a K row and joining in colours as required,
work in striped st st patt as given for Back until Left
Front matches Back to start of armhole shaping, ending
with RS facing for next row.

Shape armhole
Keeping stripes correct, cast/bind off 3 sts at beg of
next row. 24 (27:30:33) sts.
Work 1 row.
Dec 1 st at armhole edge of next and foll 3 alt rows.
20 (23:26:29) sts.
Work straight until Left Front matches Back to start of
shoulder shaping, ending with RS facing for next row.
Break off B, C and D and C and cont using A only.

Shape shoulder
Cast/bind off 4 (5:5:6) sts at beg of next and foll alt
row, then 4 (4:6:6) sts at beg of foll alt row.
Work 1 row, ending with RS facing for next row.
Break yarn and leave rem 8 (9:10:11) sts on a holder.

Right front

Using smaller pair of needles and A, cast on 27 (31:
31:35) sts.
Row 1 (RS) K3, *P2, K2, rep from * to end.
Row 2 P2, *K2, P2, rep from * to last st, K1.
These 2 rows form rib patt.
Work in rib for 6 more rows, dec (dec:inc:inc) 0 (1:2:1)
sts evenly across last row and ending with RS facing for
next row. 27 (30:33:36) sts.
Change to larger needles.
Starting with a K row and joining in colours as required,
work in striped st st patt as given for Back until Right
Front matches Back to start of armhole shaping, ending
with WS facing for next row.

Shape armhole
Keeping stripes correct, cast/bind off 3 sts at beg of
next row. 24 (27:30:33) sts.
Dec 1 st at armhole edge of next and foll 3 alt rows.
20 (23:26:29) sts.
Work straight until Right Front matches Back to start of
shoulder shaping, ending with RS facing for next row.
Break off B, C and D and cont using A only.
Work 1 row, ending with WS facing for next row.

Shape shoulder
Cast/bind off 4 (5:5:6) sts at beg of next and foll alt
row, then 4 (4:6:6) sts at beg of foll alt row, ending with
RS facing for next row.
Break yarn and leave rem 8 (9:10:11) sts on a holder.

Sleeves

Using smaller pair of needles and A, cast on 26 (30: 32:34) sts.

Work in rib as given for Back for 8 rows, inc 1 (0:1:0) st at each end of last row and ending with RS facing for next row. 28 (30:32:34) sts.

Change to larger needles.

Joining in colours as required, starting with a K row and stripe row 1, work in striped st st patt as given for Back, shaping sides by inc 1 st at each end of 3rd (3rd:3rd:5th) and foll 7 (5:0:0) alt rows, then on 0 (1:3:3) foll 4th rows. 44 (44:40:42) sts.

Work 1 (1:3:1) rows, ending after 4 rows using D and with RS facing for next row.

Break off B, C and D and cont using A only.

Inc 1 st at each end of next (3rd:next:3rd) and every foll alt (4th:4th:4th) row until there are 48 (56: 60:60) sts.

First and 4th sizes only

Inc 1 st at each end of every foll 4th (6th) row until there are 52 (64) sts.

All sizes

Work straight until Sleeve measures 16 (20:26:30)cm/ 6¼ (7¾:10¼:11¾)in, ending with RS facing for next row.

Shape top

Cast/bind off 3 sts at beg of next 2 rows. 46 (50:54:58) sts.

Dec 1 st at each end of next and foll 2 alt rows, then on foll row, ending with RS facing for next row.

Cast/bind off rem 38 (42:46:50) sts.

To finish

Press carefully following instructions on yarn label.

Sew both shoulder seams.

Hood

With RS facing, using larger needles and A, work across 8 (9:10:11) sts left on Right Front holder as follows: K4, (M1, K1) 4 (5:6:7) times, work across 20 (22:24:26) sts from Back holder as follows: K1, (M1, K1) 19 (21:23:25) times, then work across 8 (9:10:11) sts from Left Front holder as follows: (K1, M1) 4 (5:6:7) times, K4. 63 (71: 79:87) sts.

P 1 row.

Place marker on centre st of last row.

Next row (RS) K to within 1 st of marked st, M1, K3 (marked st is centre st of these 3 sts), M1, K to end.

Working in st st throughout, cont as follows:

Work 3 rows.

Rep last 4 rows twice more, then first of these rows (the inc row) again. 71 (79:87:95) sts.

Work straight until Hood measures 17 (18:19:20)cm/ 6½ (7:7½:7¾)in from pick-up row, ending with RS facing for next row.

Next row (RS) K to within 2 sts of marked st, K2tog, K marked st, sl 1, K1, psso, K to end.

P 1 row.

Rep last 2 rows twice more.

Next row (RS) K to within 2 sts of marked st, K2tog, K marked st, sl 1, K1, psso, K to end.

Next row P to within 2 sts of marked st, P2tog tbl, P marked st, P2tog, P to end.

Rep last 2 rows twice more, then work first of these rows again.

Cast/bind off rem 51 (59: 67: 75) sts.

Fold Hood in half and join cast-off/bound-off edges to form top seam of Hood.

Front and hood border

With RS facing, using circular needle and A, and starting and ending at cast-on edges, pick up and K 59 (67:77:87) sts up Right Front opening edge to Hood pick-up row, 41 (43:45:47) sts up first side of Hood to top seam, 41 (43:45:47) sts down other side of Hood to Hood pick-up row, then 59 (67:77:87) sts down Left Front opening edge. 200 (220:244:268) sts.

Row 1 (WS) K1, *P2, K2, rep from * to last 3 sts, P2, K1.

Row 2 K3, *P2, K2, rep from * to last st, K1.

These 2 rows form rib patt.

Keeping rib correct, cont as follows:

For a girl only

Row 3 (buttonhole row) (WS) Rib to last 48 (56:64:76) sts, *yrn (to make a buttonhole), work 2 tog, rib 9 (11: 13:16), rep from * 3 times more, yrn (to make 5th buttonhole), work 2 tog, rib 2.

For a boy only

Row 3 (buttonhole row) (WS) Rib 2, *work 2 tog, yrn (to make a buttonhole), rib 9 (11:13:16), rep from * 3 more times, work 2 tog, yrn (to make 5th buttonhole), rib to end.

For both a girl and a boy

Work in rib patt for 2 more rows, ending with RS facing for next row.

Cast/bind off in rib.

Matching shaped edges at underarm and centre of sleeve cast-off/bound-off edge to shoulder seam, sew sleeves into armholes. Sew side and sleeve seams. Sew on buttons.

Heart sweater

A gorgeous sweater for active little ones, which is also great fun to knit. The heart motif is knitted from a chart, using the intarsia technique. A cool cotton yarn makes the sweater comfortable even on a warm day.

Skill level

Intermediate

Techniques

- Stocking/stockinette stitch (page 19)
- Bar increases (page 28)
- Knitting or purling two stitches together (page 31)
- Following a chart (pages 66–67)
- Intarsia method (pages 62–63)
- Horizontal stripes (page 60)

Tools

1 pair of 4mm (UK 8) (US 6) knitting needles
2 stitch holders
Bobbins (see page 15)
Basic equipment for finishing (see page 35)

Materials

Rowan Handknit Cotton
3 × (3:4:5) 50g (1¾oz) balls in Sugar, 303 (**M**)

1 × (1:1:2) balls in Rosso, 215 (**A**)

1 × (1:1:2) 50g balls in Ecru, 251 (**B**)

Alternative colours
Variation 1

Decadent, 314 (**M**)

Lupin, 305 (**A**)

Ecru, 251 (**B**)

Variation 2

Ice Water, 239 (**M**)

Turkish Plum, 277 (**A**)

Bleached, 263 (**B**)

Tension/gauge

20 sts and 28 rows to 10cm/4in measured over st st using 4mm (UK 8) (US 6) needles. Change needle size if necessary to obtain correct tension/gauge.

Abbreviations

See page 6.

Measurements

Size	1	2	3	4
To fit	2–3 years	3–4 years	4–5 years	5–6 years
Chest	51cm (20in)	56cm (22in)	61cm (24in)	66cm (26in)
Actual measurements				
Chest	67cm (26½in)	73cm (28¾in)	79cm (31in)	85cm (33½in)
Length	29cm (11½in)	33cm (13in)	38cm (15in)	42cm (16½in)
Sleeve seam	18cm (7in)	21cm (8¼in)	23cm (9in)	26cm (10¼in)

Note

When changing colour always twist the yarns on the WS of your work, as explained for the intarsia technique (see pages 62–63), to avoid leaving a hole.

Back

Using yarn A, cast on 66 (74:78:86) sts.
Row 1 (RS) K2, *P2, K2, rep from * to end.
Row 2 P2, *K2, P2, rep from * to end.
These 2 rows form rib patt.
Work in rib for 7 more rows, inc (dec:inc:dec) 1 st at end of last row and ending with WS facing for next row. 67 (73:79:85) sts.
Row 10 P.
Break off A and join in M. **
Starting with a K row, work in st st until Back measures 29 (33:38:42)cm/11½ (13:15:16 ½)in, ending with RS facing for next row.

Shape shoulders and back neck

Next row (RS) Cast/bind off 18 (20:22:24) sts, K until there are 31 (33:35:37) sts on right needle, cast/bind off rem 18 (20:22:24) sts.
Break yarn and leave centre 31 (33:35:37) sts on a holder.

Front

Work as given for Back to **.
Starting with a K row, work in st st for 16 (22:30:38) rows, ending with RS facing for next row.
Next row (RS) Using M, K21 (24:27:30), K next 25 sts as row 1 of chart, reading chart from right to left, using M, K to end.
Next row Using M, P21 (24:27:30), P next 25 sts as row 2 of chart, reading chart from left to right, using M, P to end.
These 2 rows set position of chart with side sts in M.
Cont as set until all 32 rows of chart have been completed.
Starting with a K row, work in st st until 14 (14:16:16) rows fewer have been worked than on Back to start of shoulder shaping, ending with RS facing for next row.
Shape neck
Next row (RS) K27 (29:32:34) and turn, leaving rem sts on a holder.
Work each side of neck separately.
Dec 1 st at neck edge of next 8 rows, then on foll 1 (1: 2:2) alt rows. 18 (20:22:24) sts.
Work 3 rows, ending with RS facing for next row.
Shape shoulder
Cast/bind off.
With RS facing, slip centre 13 (15:15:17) sts on to a holder, rejoin yarn to rem sts, K to end.
Complete to match first side, reversing shapings.

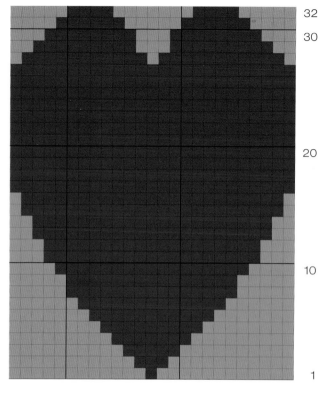

Key ▦ M ■ A

Sleeves

Using M, cast on 30 (30:34:34) sts.
Work in rib patt as given for Back for 6 rows.
Join in B.
Using B, work in rib for 2 more rows, inc 0 (1:0:1) st at each end of last row and ending with RS facing for next row. 30 (32:34:36) sts.
Starting with a K row, now work in st st throughout as follows:
Using B, work 4 rows, inc 1 st at each end of 3rd of these rows. 32 (34:36:38) sts.
Using M, work 6 rows, inc 1 st at each end of next and foll 2 (2:2:1) alt rows. 38 (40:42:42) sts.
Using B, work 6 rows, inc 1 st at each end of next (3rd: next:next) and foll alt (0:4th:4th) row. 42 (42:46:46) sts.
Last 12 rows form striped st st patt.
Cont in striped st st patt, shaping sides by inc 1 st at each end of next (next:3rd:3rd) and every foll 4th row until there are 52 (56:60:64) sts.
Work straight until Sleeve measures 18 (21:23:26)cm/ 7 (8¼:9:10¼)in, ending with RS facing for next row.
Cast/bind off.

To finish
Press carefully following instructions on yarn label. Sew right shoulder seam.

Neckband
With RS facing and using A, pick up and K 13 (13: 14:14) sts down left side of neck, K across 13 (15:15:17) sts from Front holder, pick up and K 13 (13:14:14) sts up right side of neck, then K across 31 (33:35:37) sts from Back holder. 70 (74:78:82) sts.

Starting with row 2, work in rib patt as given for Back for 6 (6:8:8) rows, ending with WS facing for next row. Cast/bind off in rib (on WS).
Sew left shoulder and neckband seam. Mark points along side seam edges 13 (14:15:16)cm/5 (5½:6:6¼)in to either side of shoulder seams and sew cast-off/bound-off edge of Sleeves to body between these points. Darn in loose ends. Sew side and sleeve seams.

Winter scarf and mittens

This cosy scarf and mittens set will keep little hands and necks nice and snug on chilly winter days while playing outdoors.

Skill level
Challenging

Techniques
- Stocking/stockinette stitch (page 19)
- Horizontal stripes (page 60)
- Stranding yarns (page 64)
- Following a chart (pages 66–67)
- Bar increases (page 28)
- Picking up stitches (page 33)
- Knitting two stitches together (page 31)
- Knitting two stitches together 'tbl' (page 31)
- Making one knit stitch (page 29)

Tools
1 pair of 4mm (UK 8) (US 6) knitting needles
Basic equipment for finishing (see page 35)

Materials
Rowan Wool Cotton
3 × 50g (1¾oz) balls in Antique, 900 (**A**)

1 × ball in Bilberry Fool, 959 (**B**)

1 × ball in Hiss, 952 (**C**)

Alternative colours
Variation 1
Antique, 900 (**A**)

Aloof, 958 (**B**)

Citron, 901 (**C**)

Variation 2
Clear, 941 (**A**)

Aloof, 958 (**B**)

Ship Shape, 955 (**C**)

Tension/gauge
22 sts and 30 rows to 10cm/4in measured over st st using 4 mm (UK 8) (US 6) needles. Change needle size if necessary to obtain correct tension/gauge.

Abbreviations
See page 6.

Notes
When changing colour on scarf, break off and rejoin yarns, leaving ends long enough for darning in later. For mittens, yarns can be carried up the side of the work.

Measurements

Size	1	2
To fit	1–2 years	3–4 years
Mittens	14 × 12.5cm (5½ × 5in)	15 × 14cm (6 × 5½in)
Scarf	20 × 117cm (8 × 46in) (for both sizes)	

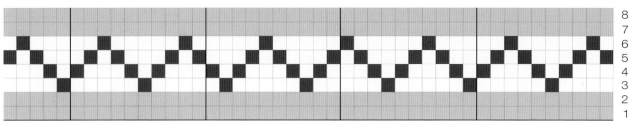

Key ☐ A ■ B ☐ C

Scarf

Using yarn B, cast on 45 sts.
Row 1 K3, *P3, K3, rep from * to end.
Row 2 P3, *K3, P3, rep from * to end.
These 2 rows form rib patt.
Change to C. Work 2 rows in rib.
Change to A. Work 2 rows in rib.
Change to B. Work 2 rows in rib.
Change to C. Work 2 rows in rib.
Change to A. Work 2 rows in rib.
Next row K.
Next row P.
These 2 rows form st st.
Work 6 more rows in st st.
Cont in patt.
**Work 8 rows from Chart.
Change to A. Work 8 rows in st st.
Change to C. Work 2 rows in st st.
Change to A. Work 2 rows in st st.
Change to B. Work 2 rows in st st.
Change to A. Work 2 rows in st st.

Change to C. Work 2 rows in st st.
Change to A. Work 2 rows in st st.
Change to B. Work 2 rows in st st.
Change to A. Work 8 rows in st st.**
The 38 rows from ** to ** form patt.
Cont in patt until scarf measures approx 110cm/43in,
finishing with Chart.
Change to A. Work 8 rows in st st.
Rib 2 rows A, C, B, A, C and B.
Cast/bind off in rib using B.

Mittens

Right mitten

**Using yarn B, cast on 30 (34) sts.
Row 1 K2, * P2, K2, rep from * to end.
Row 2 P2, * K2, P2, rep from * to end.
These 2 rows form rib patt.
Change to C.
Work 2 rows in rib.

Change to A.

Work 2 rows in rib.

Work the last 6 rows once more.

Next row (RS) K.

Next row P.

These 2 rows form st st.

Work 2 more rows in st st for second size only.**

Shape thumb

Row 1 (RS) K16 (17), M1, K1 (3), M1, K13 (14).

Work 1 (3) rows in st st.

Next row K16 (17), M1, K3 (5), M1, K13 (14).

Next row P.

Cont to inc as before on next and foll alt row.

38 (42) sts.

Next row P.

Knit thumb

Next row (RS) K 25(28), turn.

Next row P 9 (11), turn.

***Working on these 9 (11) sts , work 8 (10) rows in st st.

Next row K1, (K2tog) to end.

Break off yarn and thread through rem sts. Pull up tight and fasten off.

Sew thumb seam.

With RS facing, rejoin A to base of thumb and pick up and K 2 sts at base of thumb, then K to end. 31 (33) sts.

Next row P.

Change to C.

Work 2 rows in st st.

Change to yarns A and B.

Next row K3 (4) in A, K1 in B, *K5 in A, K1 in B, rep from * to last 3 (4) sts, K3 (4) sts in A.

Next row P2 (3) in A, P1 in B, P1 in A, P1 in B, *P3 in A, P1 in B, P1 in A, P1 in B, rep from * to last 2 (3) sts, P2 (3) in A.

Next row K1 (2) in A, K1 in B, K3 in A,* K1 in B, Kl in A, K1 in B, K3 in A, rep from * to last 2 (3) sts, K1 in B, K1 (2) in A.

Next row P0 (1) in A, P1 in B, *P5 in A, P1 in B, rep from * to last 0 (1) st, P0 (1) in A.

Work 2 rows in st st in C.

Change to A.

Next row (RS) K1, (K2tog tbl, K10 [11], K2tog, K1) twice. 27 (29) sts.

Next row P.

Next row K1, (K2tog tbl, K 8 [9], K2tog, K1) twice. 23 (25) sts.

Next row P.

Next row K1, (K2tog tbl, K6 [7], K2tog, K1) twice. 19 (21) sts.

Cast/bind off.

Left mitten

Work as for Right Mitten from ** to **.

Shape thumb

Row 1 (RS) K13 (14), M1, K1 (3), M1, K16 (17).

Work 1 (3) rows in st st.

Next row K13 (14), M1, K3 (5), M1, K16 (17).

Next row P.

Cont to inc as before on next and foll alt row.

38 (42) sts.

Next row P.

Knit thumb

Next row (RS) K22 (25), turn.

Next row P9 (11), turn.

Now work from *** to end as for Right Mitten.

To finish

Block scarf or press lightly, following instructions on yarn label. Darn in loose ends.

Block mittens. Darn in loose ends. Sew seams using backstitch or an edge-to-edge seam.

Tassel hat

This droll little hat, with its perky tassels, is sure to look great on little ones. And, as there is no shaping to do, it is very simple to make!

Skill level
Easy

Techniques
- Stocking/stockinette stitch (page 19)
- Moss/seed stitch (page 168)
- Darning in ends (page 37)
- Seams (page 36)
- Tassels (page 75)

Tools
1 pair of 3.25mm (UK 10) (US 3) knitting needles
1 pair of 3.75mm (UK 9) (US 5) knitting needles
Basic equipment for finishing (see page 35)

Materials
Jaeger Matchmaker Merino DK

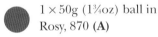 1 × 50g (1¾oz) ball in Rosy, 870 (**A**)

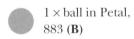 1 × ball in Petal, 883 (**B**)

Alternative colours

Mariner, 629 **A**

Feather, 864 **B**

Tension/gauge
23 sts and 30 rows to 10cm/4in measured over st st using 3.75mm (UK 9) (US 5) needles. Change needle size if necessary to obtain correct tension/gauge.

Abbreviations
See page 6.

Hat
Using larger needles and A, cast on 49 (53:57) sts.
Row 1 (RS) K1, *P1, K1, rep from * to end.
Row 2 P1, *K1, P1, rep from * to end.
These 2 rows form moss/seed st patt.
Work in moss/seed st for 16 (19:19) more rows.
Change to smaller needles.
Work in moss/seed st for 18 (21: 21) more rows, ending with RS facing for next row.
Break off A and join in B.
Change to larger needles.
Starting with a K row, work in st st until Hat measures 30 (35:39)cm/ 11¾ (13¾:15¼)in, ending with WS facing for next row.
Break off B and join in A.
Change to smaller needles.
Next row P.
Work in moss/seed st for 18 (21: 21) rows.
Change to larger needles.
Work in moss/seed st for 18 (21:21) more rows more, ending with RS facing for next row.
Cast/bind off in moss/seed st.

To finish
Press carefully following instructions on yarn label. Darn in loose ends.
Fold Hat in half, matching cast-on and cast-off/bound-off edges, and sew side seams, reversing seam for section in B for turn-back. Fold turn-back to outside. Using A, make two 8cm/3in-long tassels and sew to corners of Hat as shown in photograph.

Measurements

Size	1	2	3
To fit	1–2 years	3–4 years	5–6 years
Actual measurements			
Around head	43cm (17in)	46cm (18in)	50cm (19½in)

Here are five cosy winter warmers for teenagers and adults. Each of the projects is suitable for a man or woman and they all make ideal gifts – simply change the colours to reflect personal taste and preference. Skill level ranges from easy to challenging, so you might be better starting with the head-turning hat and scarf before trying the more complex striped toasty gloves. For intermediate skill, try the cable-fronted pullover or a basic slouchy sweater. The socks are fun and include an optional embroidered element.

Gorgeous for grown-ups

Single cable pullover

Knitted in a robust pure wool yarn, this sweater is an ideal top layer when the temperature drops. The simple cable down the front makes it a good project if you're trying cables for the first time.

Skill level

Intermediate

Techniques

- Stocking/stockinette stitch (page 19)
- Bar increases (page 28)
- Knitting or purling two stitches together (page 31)
- Cables (page 40)
- Picking up stitches (page 33)
- Seams (page 36)

Tools

1 pair of 7mm (UK 2) (US 10½) knitting needles
1 pair of 8mm (UK 0) (US 11) knitting needles
1 cable needle
1 stitch holder
Basic equipment for finishing (see page 35)

Materials

Rowan Scottish Tweed Chunky
9 × (9:10:10:11) 100g (3½oz) balls in Sea Green, 006 **(A)**

1 × ball in Seaspray, 034 **(B)**

Alternative colours

Variation 1

Oatmeal, 025 **(A)**

Olive Green, 035 **(B)**

Variation 2

Lobster, 017 **(A)**

Porridge, 024 **(B)**

Tension/gauge

12 sts and 16 rows to 10cm/4in measured over st st using 8mm (UK 0) (US 11) needles. Change needle size if necessary to obtain correct tension/gauge.

Abbreviations

See page 6.

Measurements

Size	1	2	3	4	5
To fit chest	97cm (38in)	102cm (40in)	107cm (42in)	112cm (44in)	117cm (46in)
Actual measurements					
Chest	112cm (44in)	118cm (46½in)	122cm (48in)	128cm (50½in)	132cm (52in)
Length	66cm (26in)	67cm (26½in)	68cm (26¾in)	69cm (27¼in)	70cm (27½in)
Sleeve seam	48cm (19in)	49cm (19¼in)	49cm (19¼in)	50cm (19¾in)	50cm (19¾in)

Back

Using smaller needles and yarn A, cast on 66 (70:
74:78:78) sts.
Row 1 (RS) K2, *P2, K2, rep from * to end.
Row 2 P2, *K2, P2, rep from * to end.
These 2 rows form rib patt.
Join in B.
Keeping rib patt correct, work in stripes as follows:
Rows 3 and 4 Using B.
Rows 5 and 6 Using A.
Rows 7–10 Rep rows 3–6.
Row 11 Using B.
Row 12 Using B, inc (inc:dec:dec:inc) 1 st at end of
row. 67 (71:73:77:79) sts.
Break off B and cont using A only.
Change to larger needles. **
Starting with a K row, work in st st until Back measures
41cm/16in, ending with RS facing for next row.
Shape armholes
Cast/bind off 3 sts at beg of next 2 rows. 61 (65:67:
71:73) sts.
Dec 1 st at each end of next 5 rows, then on foll 2 (3:
3:4:4) alt rows. 47 (49:51:53:55) sts.
Work straight until armhole measures 25 (26:
27:28:29)cm/9¾ (10¼:10½:11:11½in), ending with RS
facing for next row.
Shape shoulders and back neck
Next row (RS) Cast/bind off 6 (7:7:7:7) sts, K until
there are 10 (10:10:11:11) sts on right needle and turn,
leaving rem sts on a holder.
Work each side of neck separately.
Cast/bind off 3 sts at beg of next row.
Cast/bind off rem 7 (7:7:8:8) sts.
With RS facing, rejoin yarn to rem sts, cast/bind off
centre 15 (15:17:17:19) sts, K to end.
Complete to match first side, reversing shapings.

Front

Work as given for Back to **.
Next row (RS) K27 (29:30:32:33), P1, inc purlwise in
next st, P1, K3, inc knitwise in next st, K3, P1, inc
purlwise in next st, P1, K to end. 70 (74:76:80:82) sts.
Cont in cable patt as follows:
Row 1 (WS) P27 (29:30:32:33), K4, P8, K4, P to end.
Row 2 K27 (29:30:32:33), P4, K8, P4, K to end.
Rows 3–10 (Rep rows 1 and 2) 4 times.
Row 11 Rep row 1.
Row 12 K27 (29:30:32:33), P4, slip next 4 sts on to cable
needle and leave at back of work, K4, then K4 from
cable needle, P4, K to end.

Rows 13–16 (Rep rows 1 and 2) twice.
These 16 rows form cable patt.
Cont in cable patt until Front matches Back to start of
armhole shaping, ending with RS facing for next row.
Shape armholes
Keeping patt correct, cast/bind off 3 sts at beg of next
2 rows. 64 (68:70:74:76) sts.
Dec 1 st at each end of next 5 rows, then on foll 2 (3:3:
4:4) alt rows. 50 (52:54:56:58) sts.
Work straight until 12 (12:14:14:14) rows fewer have
been worked than on Back to start of shoulder shaping,
ending with RS facing for next row.
Shape neck
Next row (RS) Patt 19 (20:21:22:22) sts and turn,
leaving rem sts on a holder.
Work each side of neck separately.
Keeping patt correct, dec 1 st at neck edge of next
4 rows, then on foll 2 (2:3:3:3) alt rows. 13 (14:14:
15:15) sts.
Work 3 rows, ending with RS facing for next row.
Shape shoulder
Cast/bind off 6 (7:7:7:7) sts at beg of next row.
Work 1 row.
Cast/bind off rem 7 (7:7:8:8) sts.
With RS facing, rejoin yarn to rem sts, cast/bind off
centre 12 (12:12:12:14) sts, patt to end.
Complete to match first side, reversing shapings.

Sleeves

Using smaller needles and A, cast on 30 (30:34:
34:34) sts.
Work rows 1–11 as given for Back.
Row 12 Using B, inc (inc:dec:inc:inc) 1 st at end of row.
31 (31:33:35:35) sts.
Break off B and cont using A only.
Change to larger needles.
Starting with a K row, work in st st, shaping sides by inc
1 st at each end of 3rd and every foll 4th row to 35 (39:
41:41:47) sts, then on every foll 6th row until there are
51 (53:55:57:59) sts.
Work straight until Sleeve measures 48 (49:49:
50:50)cm/19 (19¼:19¼:19¾:19¾)in, ending with RS
facing for next row.
Shape top
Cast/bind off 3 sts at beg of next 2 rows. 45 (47:49:
51:53) sts.
Dec 1 st at each end of next 3 rows, then on every foll
alt row to 21 sts, then on foll 5 rows, ending with RS
facing for next row.
Cast/bind off rem 11 sts.

To finish

Press carefully following instructions on yarn label.
Darn in loose ends.
Sew right shoulder seam.

Neckband

With RS facing, using smaller needles and A, pick up
and K 12 (12:13:15:15) sts down left side of neck,
9 (9:9:9:11) sts from front neck, 12 (12:13:15:15) sts
up right side of neck, then 21 (21:23:23:25) sts from
back neck. 54 (54:58:62:66) sts.

Work in rib patt as given for Back for 2 rows.
Join in B.
Using B, work in rib for 2 rows.
Break off B.
Using A, work in rib for 2 more rows, ending with WS
facing for next row.
Cast/bind off **loosely** in rib (on WS).
Sew left shoulder and neckband seam. Sew side seams.
Sew sleeve seams. Sew in sleeves.

Slouchy sweater

This pullover is extremely versatile and can be worn for work or leisure. Knit it in a colour to complement your favourite trousers or skirt.

Skill level

Intermediate

Techniques

- Stocking/stockinette stitch (page 19)
- Knitting or purling two stitches together (page 31)
- Bar increases (page 28)
- Picking up stitches (page 33)
- Darning in ends (page 37)
- Seams (page 36)

Tools

1 pair of 4mm (UK 8) (US 6) knitting needles
2 stitch holders
2 stitch markers
Basic equipment for finishing (see page 35)

Materials

Rowan Scottish Tweed DK
15 × (16:17) 50g (1¾oz) balls in Porridge, 024

Tension/gauge

20 sts and 28 rows to 10cm/4in measured over st st using 4mm (UK 8) (US 6) needles. Change needle size if necessary to obtain correct tension/gauge.

Abbreviations

See page 6.

Measurements

Size	1	2	3
To fit bust/chest	81–86cm (32–34in)	91–97cm (36–38in)	102–107cm (40–42in)
Actual measurements			
Bust/chest	128cm (50½in)	134cm (52¾in)	40cm (55in)
Length	69cm (27in)	71cm (28in)	73cm (28¾in)
Sleeve seam	41cm (16in)	41cm (16in)	42cm (16½in)

Back

Cast on 128 (134:140) sts.
Row 1 (RS) K2, *P1, K2, rep from * to end.
Row 2 P2, *K1, P2, rep from * to end.
These 2 rows form rib patt.
Work in rib until Back measures 8cm/3in, ending with RS facing for next row.
Starting with a K row, work in st st until Back measures 45 (46:47)cm/17¾ (18:18½)in, ending with RS facing for next row.
Shape armholes
Cast/bind off 9 sts at beg of next 2 rows. 110 (116: 122) sts.
Work straight until armhole measures 24 (25:26)cm/ 9½ (9¾:10¼)in, ending with RS facing for next row.
Shape shoulders and back neck
Cast/bind) off 19 (20:21) sts at beg of next 2 rows, then 19 (21:22) sts at beg of foll 2 rows.
Break yarn and leave rem 34 (34:36) sts on a holder.

Front

Work as given for Back until 12 (12:14) rows fewer have been worked than on Back to start of shoulder shaping, ending with RS facing for next row.
Shape neck
Next row (RS) K46 (49:52) and turn, leaving rem sts on a holder.
Work each side of neck separately.
Dec 1 st at neck edge of next 6 rows, then on foll 2 (2:3) alt rows. 38 (41:43) sts.
Work 1 row, ending with RS facing for next row.
Shape shoulder
Cast/bind off 19 (20:21) sts at beg of next row.
Work 1 row.
Cast/bind off rem 19 (21:22) sts.
With RS facing, slip centre 18 sts on to a holder, rejoin yarn to rem sts, K to end.
Complete to match first side, reversing shapings.

Sleeves

Cast on 65 (68:71) sts.
Work in rib patt as given for Back for 8cm/3in, ending with WS facing for next row.
First size only Work 1 row, inc 1 st at end of row. 66 sts.
Second size only Work 1 row.
Third size only Work 1 row, dec. 1 st at end of last row. 70 sts.
All sizes Starting with a K row, work in st st, shaping sides by inc 1 st at each end of 3rd and every foll 4th row to 74 (82:88) sts, then on every foll 6th row until there are 96 (100:104) sts.
Work straight until Sleeve measures 41 (41:42)cm/

16 (16:16½)in, ending with RS facing for next row.
Shape top
Place markers at both ends of last row to denote top of sleeve seam.
Work 12 more rows, ending with RS facing for next row.
Cast/bind off.

To finish

Press carefully following instructions on yarn label. Sew right shoulder seam.
Neckband
With RS facing, pick up and K 13 (13:15) sts down left side of neck, K across 18 sts from front holder, pick up and K 12 (12:14) sts up right side of neck, then K across 34 (34:36) sts from back holder. 77 (77:83) sts.
Starting with row 2, work in rib patt as given for Back for 8cm/3in, ending with RS facing for next row.
Cast/bind off in rib.
Sew left shoulder and neckband seam. Matching sleeve markers to top of side seams, shaped edges at underarm and centre of sleeve cast-off/bound-off edge to shoulder seam, sew sleeves into armholes. Darn in loose ends. Sew side and sleeve seams.

Toasty warm gloves

A soft yet practical pair of gloves, with or without fingers, that can be knitted in bright stripes or a solid colour.

Skill level
Challenging

Techniques
- Stocking/stockinette stitch (page 19)
- Casting/binding off in rib (page 21)
- Horizontal stripes (page 60)
- Making one knit stitch (page 29)
- Multiple increase (page 81)
- Knitting two stitches together (page 31)
- Seams (page 36)
- Picking up stitches (page 33)

Tools
1 pair of 3.75mm (UK 9) (US 5) knitting needles
Basic equipment for finishing (see page 35)

Materials

Striped gloves
Rowan RYC Cashsoft DK 1 × 50g (1¾oz) ball in Poppy, 512 **(A)**

1 × ball in Clementine, 510 **(B)**

Alternative colours
Variation 1
Navy, 514 **(A)**

Mist, 505 **(B)**

Variation 2
Bloom, 520 **(A)**

Sweet, 501 **(B)**

Fingerless gloves
Rowan RYC Cashsoft DK 2 × 50g (1¾oz) balls in your chosen colour

Tension/gauge
23 sts and 31 rows to 10cm/4in measured over st st using 3.75mm (UK 9) (US 5) needles. Change needle size if necessary to obtain correct tension/gauge.

Abbreviations
See page 6.

Notes
When rejoining yarn for thumb and fingers, leave a tail long enough for sewing the seam. For a smooth, comfortable finish, use the edge-to-edge seam shown on page 36.

Measurements

Size	1	2
To fit an average-size hand	woman's	man's
Actual measurements		
Around hand	21cm (8¼in)	24cm (9½in)

Striped gloves

Right glove
Using A, cast on 48 (56) sts.
Row 1 WS Using A, *K1, P1, rep from * to end.
Join in B.
Rows 2 and 3 Using B, *K1, P1, rep from * to end.
Row 4 Rep row 1.
Rep last 4 rows 2 (3) more times, ending with RS facing for next row.
Now work in striped st st as follows:
Row 1 (RS) Using A, K.
Row 2 Using B, P.
Row 3 Using B, K.
Row 4 Using A, P.
These 4 rows form striped st st patt.***
Keeping stripes correct throughout, cont as follows:
Shape thumb gusset
Row 1 (RS) K25 (29), M1, K1, M1, K to end. 50 (58) sts.
Work 3 rows.
Row 5 K25 (29), M1, K3, M1, K to end. 52 (60) sts.
Work 3 rows.
Row 9 K25 (29), M1, K5, M1, K to end. 54 (62) sts.
Work 3 rows.
Row 13 K25 (29), M1, K7, M1, K to end. 56 (64) sts.
Work 3 rows.
Row 17 K25 (29), M1, K9, M1, K to end. 58 (66) sts.
Man's size only
Work 3 rows.
Row 21 K29, M1, K11, M1, K to end. 68 sts.
Both sizes
Work 1 row, ending with RS facing for next row.
Shape thumb
Next row (RS) K37 (43) and turn.
****Next row** Cast on and P 3 sts, P13 (15) and turn.
Work 16 (18) rows on these 16 (18) sts only for thumb, ending with RS facing for next row.
Next row (RS) K1 (0), (K2tog, K1) 5 (6) times. 11 (12) sts.
Next row P.
Next row K1 (0), (K2tog) 5 (6) times.
Break yarn and thread through rem 6 sts. Pull up tight and fasten off securely. Sew thumb seam.
Shape hand
With RS facing, rejoin appropriate yarn at base of thumb, pick up and K 3 sts from thumb cast-on edge, K to end. 48 (56) sts.
Work 11 (13) rows, ending with RS facing for next row.
Shape first finger
Next row (RS) K30 (35) and turn.
Next row Inc in first st, P11 (13), inc in next st and turn.
Work 20 (22) rows on these 15 (17) sts only for first finger, ending with RS facing for next row.
Next row (RS) K0 (2), (K2tog, K1) 5 times.

10 (12) sts.
Next row P.
Next row (K2tog) 5 (6) times.
Break yarn and thread through rem 5 (6) sts. Pull up tight and fasten off securely. Sew seam.**
Shape second finger
With RS facing, rejoin appropriate yarn at base of first finger, pick up and K 2 sts from base of first finger, K6 (7) and turn.
Next row (WS) Inc in first st, P11 (13), inc in next st and turn.
Work 22 (24) rows on these 15 (17) sts only for second finger, ending with RS facing for next row.
Complete as for first finger from ** to **.
Shape third finger
With RS facing, rejoin appropriate yarn at base of second finger, pick up and K 2 sts from base of second finger, K6 (7) and turn.
Next row (WS) Inc in first st, P11 (13), inc in next st and turn.
Work 20 (22) rows on these 15 (17) sts only for third finger, ending with RS facing for next row.
Complete as for first finger from ** to **.
Shape fourth finger
With RS facing, rejoin appropriate yarn at base of third finger, pick up and K 2 sts from base of third finger, K to end.
Work 17 (19) rows on these 15 (17) sts only for fourth finger, ending with RS facing for next row.
Complete as for first finger from ** to **.

Left glove
Work as given for Right Glove to ***.
Keeping stripes correct throughout, cont as follows:
Shape thumb gusset
Row 1 (RS) K22 (26), M1, K1, M1, K to end. 50 (58) sts.
Work 3 rows.
Row 5 K22 (26), M1, K3, M1, K to end. 52 (60) sts.
Work 3 rows.
Row 9 K22 (26), M1, K5, M1, K to end. 54 (62) sts.
Work 3 rows.
Row 13 K22 (26), M1, K7, M1, K to end. 56 (64) sts.
Work 3 rows.
Row 17 K22 (26), M1, K9, M1, K to end. 58 (66) sts.
Man's size only
Work 3 rows.
Row 21 K26, M1, K11, M1, K to end. 68 sts.
Both sizes
Work 1 row, ending with RS facing for next row.
Shape thumb
Next row (RS) K34 (40) and turn.
Complete as given for Right Glove from **** to end.

To finish

Darn in loose ends. Press carefully following instructions on yarn label.

Fingerless gloves

Right glove

Using same colour throughout, work as given for Right Striped Glove to start of thumb shaping.

Shape thumb

Next row (RS) K37 (43) and turn.

*****Next row** Cast on and P 3 sts, P13 (15) and turn. 16 (18) sts.

Next row *K1, P1, rep from * to end.

Rep last row 3 more times, ending with RS facing for next row.

Cast/bind off in rib.

Sew thumb seam.

Shape hand

With RS facing, rejoin yarn at base of thumb, pick up and K 3 sts from thumb cast-on edge, K to end. 48 (56) sts.

Work 11 (13) rows, ending with RS facing for next row.

Shape first finger

Next row (RS) K30 (35) and turn.

Next row Inc in first st, P11 (13), inc in next st and turn. 15 (17) sts.

Next row (RS) K1, *P1, K1, rep from * to end.

Next row P1, *K1, P1, rep from * to end.

Rep last 2 rows once more.

Cast/bind off in rib.

Sew seam.

Shape second finger

With RS facing, rejoin yarn at base of first finger, pick up and K 2 sts from base of first finger, K6 (7) and turn.

Next row (WS) Inc in first st, P11 (13), inc in next st and turn. 15 (17) sts.

Next row (RS) K1, *P1, K1, rep from * to end.

Next row P1, *K1, P1, rep from * to end.

Rep last 2 rows once more.

Cast/bind off in rib.

Sew seam.

Shape third finger

With RS facing, rejoin yarn at base of second finger, pick up and K 2 sts from base of second finger, K6 (7) and turn.

Next row (WS) Inc in first st, P11 (13), inc in next st and turn. 15 (17) sts.

Next row (RS) K1, *P1, K1, rep from * to end.

Next row P1, *K1, P1, rep from * to end.

Rep last 2 rows once more.

Cast/bind off in rib.

Sew seam.

Shape fourth finger

With RS facing, rejoin yarn at base of third finger, pick up and K 2 sts from base of third finger, K to end. 15 (17) sts.

Next row (WS) P.

Next row K1, *P1, K1, rep from * to end.

Next row P1, *K1, P1, rep from * to end.

Rep last 2 rows once more.

Cast/bind off in rib.

Sew seam.

Left glove

Using same colour throughout, work as given for Right Striped Glove to ***.

Shape thumb gusset

Row 1 (RS) K22 (26), M1, K1, M1, K to end. 50 (58) sts.

Work 3 rows.

Row 5 K22 (26), M1, K3, M1, K to end. 52 (60) sts.

Work 3 rows.

Row 9 K22 (26), M1, K5, M1, K to end. 54 (62) sts.

Work 3 rows.

Row 13 K22 (26), M1, K7, M1, K to end. 56 (64) sts.

Work 3 rows.

Row 17 K22 (26), M1, K9, M1, K to end. 58 (66) sts.

Man's size only

Work 3 rows.

Row 21 K26, M1, K11, M1, K to end. 68 sts.

Both sizes

Work 1 row, ending with RS facing for next row.

Shape thumb

Next row (RS) K34 (40) and turn.

Complete as given for Right Fingerless Glove from ***** to end.

To finish

Darn in loose ends. Press carefully following instructions on yarn label.

Head-turning hat and scarf

You'll be amazed at just how quick these are to knit – which makes them ideal gifts for all your friends and family!

Skill level
Easy

Techniques
- Horizontal stripes (page 60)
- Knitting two stitches together (page 31)
- Darning in ends (page 37)
- Seams (page 36)

Tools
1 pair of 9mm (UK 00) (US 13) knitting needles
Basic equipment for finishing (see page 35)

Materials

Woman's hat
Rowan Little Big Wool
1 × 50g (1¾oz) ball in Onyx, 501 (**A**)

1 × ball in Garnet, 503 (**B**)

1 × ball in Amethyst, 504 (**C**)

Man's hat
Rowan Little Big Wool
1 × 50g (1¾oz) ball in Moonstone, 507 (**A**)

1 × ball in Topaz, 509 (**B**)

Woman's scarf
Rowan Little Big Wool
1 × 50g (1¾oz) ball in Onyx, 501 (**A**)

2 × balls in Garnet, 503 (**B**)

2 × balls in Amethyst, 504 (**C**)

Man's scarf
Rowan Little Big Wool
1 × 50g (1¾oz) ball in Moonstone, 507 (**A**)

4 × balls in Topaz, 509 (**B**)

Tension/gauge
11 sts and 15 rows to 10cm/4in measured over st st using 9mm (UK 00) (US 13) needles. Change needle size if necessary to obtain correct tension/gauge.

Abbreviations
See page 6.

Notes
When changing colour on Hat, carry unused yarn up side edge. On Scarf, break off and rejoin yarns at each colour change.

Measurements – Hat

Size	1	2
To fit an average-size head	woman's	man's
Actual measurements		
Around lower edge	56cm (22in)	59cm (23¼in)

Measurements – Scarf

Finished size	20 × 150cm (8 × 59in)

Hat

Using yarn A, cast on 62 (65) sts.
Row 1 K.
Row 2 K.
These 2 rows form garter st.
Change to B.
Row 3 K.
Row 4 P.
These 2 rows form st st.
Work 2 more rows in st st.
Woman's hat only
Change to A.
Work 2 rows garter st.
Change to C.
Work 4 rows in st st.
These 12 rows form stripe patt.
Cont in stripe patt until work measures 13cm/5in, ending with RS facing for next row.
Man's hat only
Using B throughout work as for Woman's Hat until work measures 14.5cm/5¾in, ending with RS facing for next row.
Shape top (both hats)
Cont in stripe patt for Woman's Hat or solid colour for Man's Hat shape top as follows:
Next row (RS) K2 (5), *K2tog, K3, rep from * to end. 50 (53) sts.
Work 3 rows.
Next row K2 (5), *K2tog, K2, rep from * to end. 38 (41) sts.
Work 3 rows.
Next row K2 (5), *K2tog, K1, rep from * to end. 26 (29)sts.
Work 1 row.
Next row K 0 (1), K2tog across the row. 13 (15) sts.
Break off yarn and thread through rem 13 (15) sts. Pull up tight and fasten off.

To finish hat

Block the work. Darn in loose ends. Sew back seam using backstitch or edge-to-edge seam.

Woman's scarf

Using A, cast on 22 sts.
Row 1 K.
Row 2 K.
These 2 rows form garter st.
Change to B.
Row 3 K.
Row 4 P.
These 2 rows form st st.
Work 2 more rows in st st.
Change to A.
Work 2 rows garter st.
Change to C.
Work 4 rows st st.
These 12 rows form the stripe patt.
Rep stripe patt until scarf measures 150cm/59in, ending with 2 rows of garter st.
Cast/bind off.

Man's scarf

Using A, cast on 22 sts.
Work 2 rows in garter st.
Change to B.
Work as for Woman's Scarf, but using B throughout, until work measures 150cm/59in, ending with 4 rows of st st in B.
Change to A.
Work 2 rows garter stitch.
Cast/bind off.

To finish scarf

Block the work. Darn in loose ends.

Super socks

The yarn for these socks has a slight stretch to it, which makes for a snug fit. Add an embroidered motif, if you like, for extra style.

Skill level
Challenging

Techniques
- Tubular fabric on double-pointed needles (page 52)
- Stocking/stockinette stitch (page 19)
- Knitting or purling two stitches together (page 31)
- Slipped stitch decrease (page 32)
- Turning a heel (pages 54–55)
- Picking up stitches (page 33)
- Double cast-/bind-off (page 83)
- Embroidery on knitting (page 71)

Tools
1 set of 4 double-pointed 3.75mm (UK 9) (US 5) knitting needles
1 stitch holder
1 blunt-ended yarn needle
Basic equipment for finishing (see page 35)

Materials
Rowan Calmer
3 × 50g (1¾oz) balls in Refresh, 487

Small amount in Drift, 460, for optional embroidery

Alternative colours
Variation 1
 Slosh, 479

Variation 2
Powder Puff, 482

Tension/gauge
23 sts and 34 rows to 10cm/4in measured over st st using 3.75mm (UK 9) (US 5) needles. Change needle size if necessary to obtain correct tension/gauge.

Abbreviations
See page 6.

Note
The method of turning a heel shown on pages 54–55 differs slightly from the one used in this pattern, but the principle is basically the same.

Measurements

Sizes	1	2
To fit an average-size foot	woman's	man's
Actual measurements		
Length	22cm (8½in)	24cm (9½in)

Socks

Cast on 54 (60) sts.

Distribute these sts over 3 of the needles and, using 4th needle, work in rounds as follows:

Round 1 (RS) *K2, P1, rep from * to end.

Rep this round 5 more times, inc (dec) 1 st at end of last round. 55 (59) sts.

Round 7 K.

This round forms st st.

Cont in rounds of st st until Sock measures 20 (21)cm/ 7¾ (8¼)in.

Next round K12 (13), K2tog, K1, sl 1, K1, psso, K to end. 53 (57) sts.

Work straight until Sock measures 25 (27)cm/ 9¾ (10½)in.

Next round K11 (12), K2tog, K1, sl 1, K1, psso, K to end. 51 (55) sts.

Work straight until Sock measures 30 (33)cm/ 11¾ (13)in.

Shape heel

Next round K25 (27) and turn.

Slip rem 26 (28) sts on to a holder and now work backwards and forwards in rows, not rounds, on these 25 (27) sts only for heel.

Starting with a P row, work in st st for 11 (13) rows, ending with RS facing for next row.

Next row K17 (18), sl 1, K1, psso and turn.

Next row P10, P2tog and turn.

Next row K10, sl 1, K1, psso and turn.

Rep last 2 rows 5 (6) more times, then first of these 2 rows again, ending with RS facing for next row. 11 sts. Break off yarn.

Shape instep

With RS facing, rejoin yarn at base of heel and pick up and K 7 (8) sts up first row-end edge of heel, K across 11 heel sts, pick up and K 7 (8) sts down other row-end edge of heel, then K across 26 (28) sts left on holder. 51 (55) sts.

Distribute these sts over 3 of the needles and, using 4th needle, work in rounds as follows:

Next round K 0 (1), (P1, K2) 8 times, P1, K to end.

Rep this round until foot measures 18 (20)cm/7 (7¾)in from back of heel.

Shape toe

Round 1 K 0 (1), (P1, K2) 4 times, K2tog, K1, (P1, K2) 3 times, P1, K1 (2), sl 1, K1, psso, K to last 3 sts, K2tog, K1. 48 (52) sts.

Round 2 K.

Round 3 (K1, sl 1, K1, psso, K18 [20], K2tog, K1) twice. 44 (48) sts.

Round 4 K.

Round 5 (K1, sl 1, K1, psso, K16 [18], K2tog, K1) twice. 40 (44) sts.

Round 6 K.

Round 7 (K1, sl 1, K1, psso, K14 [16], K2tog, K1) twice. 36 (40) sts.

Round 8 K.

Round 9 (K1, sl 1, K1, psso, K12 [14], K2tog, K1) twice. 32 (36) sts.

Round 10 K.

Round 11 (K1, sl 1, K1, psso, K10 [12], K2tog, K1) twice. 28 (32) sts.

Round 12 K.

Round 13 (K1, sl 1, K1, psso, K8 [10], K2tog, K1) twice. 24 (28) sts.

Round 14 K.

Slip first 12 (14) sts on to one needle and other 12 (14) sts on to another needle.

Turn Sock inside out and fold toe flat. Using a 3rd needle, cast/bind off both sets of 12 (14) sts together, taking one st from first needle along with corresponding st from 2nd needle.

To finish

Press carefully following instructions on yarn label.

Embroidery (optional)

Following photograph as a guide, embroider design on side of Sock using contrasting yarn and blunt-ended yarn needle. For flowers, work 5 or 6 individual chain stitches radiating out from one point (lazy daisy stitch), and embroider a French knot at centre. Add a few single chain stitch leaves sprinkled around flowers.

All women love bags, and among the projects here you will find a fab felted bag and a pretty, easy-to-make tote bag, both of which make a worthy addition to any collection. For homemakers the squishy cushion has a versatile chequered pattern and an optional lacy edging. There is also a fabulous blanket made of individual knitted squares, which means you can make it in any size or arrangement you like. The chapter ends with an irresistibly cute knitted bunny – without which any book on knitting would be incomplete.

Accessories for everyone

Fab felted bag

Felting this bag after you've knitted it gives a really firm fabric so that the bag will keep its shape and can take more weight without stretching.

Skill level
Intermediate

Techniques
- Stocking/stockinette stitch (page 19)
- Bar increase (page 28)
- Making one knit stitch (page 29)
- Stranding yarns (page 64)

Tools
1 pair of 4mm (UK 8) (US 6) knitting needles
Basic equipment for finishing (see page 35)

Materials
Rowan Scottish Tweed DK
3 × 50g (1¾oz) balls in Oatmeal, 25 (**A**)

1 × ball in Apple, 15 (**C**)

1 × ball in Thatch, 18 (**B**)

1 × ball in Peat, 19 (**D**)

Alternative colours
Variation 1
Thistle, 16 (**A**)

Purple Heather, 30 (**B**)

Lavender, 5 (**C**)

Skye, 3 (**D**)

Variation 2
Lewis Grey, 7 (**A**)

Grey Mist, 1 (**B**)

Stormy Grey, 4 (**C**)

Indigo, 31 (**D**)

1 button

Tension/gauge
22 sts and 30 rows to 10cm/4in measured over st st using 4mm (UK 8) (US 6) needles, before felting. Change needle size if necessary to obtain correct tension/gauge.

Abbreviations
See page 6.

Notes
When changing to a new colour of yarn, do not break off the previous yarn unless instructed otherwise. If you wish to knit the back of the bag in a single colour, work as for the front but using one colour yarn throughout. You will need 4 balls of yarn in total.

Measurements
Finished size approximately 21 × 26cm (8¼ × 10¼in) when felted. (Size may vary, as each washing machine is different and will felt each bag differently.)

Front

Using yarn A, cast on 25 sts.
Row 1 K.
Row 2 P.
These 2 rows form st st.
Cont in st st and at the same time inc 1 st at each end of next and every row until there are 37 sts.
Change to B.
Next row K1, M1, K to last st, M1, K1. 39 sts
Next row P1, M1, P to last st, M1, P1. 41 sts
Next row K1, M1 in B, K3 in A, *K3 in B, K3 in A, rep from * to last st, M1, K1 in B.
Next row P2 in B, P3 in A, *P3 in B, P3 in A, rep from * to last 2 sts, P2 in B.
Next row K1, M1, K1 in B, K3 in A, *K3 in B, K3 in A, rep from * to last 2 sts, K1, M1, K1 in B.
Next row P3 in B, *P3 in A, P3 in B, rep from * to end.
Work 2 rows st st in B inc 1 st at each end of next row.
Break off B.
Work 6 rows st st in A inc 1 st at each end of next and foll 2 alt rows. 53 sts.
Change to C.
Work 2 rows st st in C inc 1 st at each end of next row.
Next row K2 in C, K3 in A, *K3 in C, K3 in A, rep from * to last 2 sts, K2 in C.
Next row P2 in C, P3 in A, *P3 in C, P3 in A, rep from * to last 2 sts, P2 in C.
Next row K1, M1, K1 in C, K3 in A, *K3 in C, K3 in A, rep from * to last 2 sts, K1, M1, K1 in C. 57 sts.
Next row P3 in C, *P3 in A, P3 in C, rep from * to end.
Work 2 rows st st in C.
Break off C.
Work 6 rows st st in A.
Change to D.
Work 2 rows st st in D.
Next row K3 in D, *K3 in A, K3 in D, rep from * to end.
Next row P3 in D, *P3 in A, P3 in D, rep from * to end.
Rep last 2 rows once more.
Work 2 rows st st in D.
Break off D.
Work 6 rows st st in A.
Change to B.
Work 2 rows st st in B.
Next row K3 in B, *K3 in A, K3 in B, rep from * to end.
Next row P3 in B, *P3 in A, P3 in B, rep from * to end.
Rep last 2 rows once more.
Work 2 rows st st in B.
Break off B.
Work 6 rows st st in A.
Change to C.
Work 2 rows st st in C.
Next row K3 in C, *K3 in A, K3 in C, rep from * to end.
Next row P3 in C, *P3 in A, P3 in C, rep from * to end.
Rep last 2 rows once more.
Work 2 rows st st in C.
Break off C.
Work 6 rows st st in A.
Cast/bind off.

Back

Work as for Front.
If you want a solid-colour Back, work as for Front but using one colour throughout.

Handle

Using A, cast on 15 sts.
Work in st st until handle measures 140cm/55in in length.
Cast/bind off.

To finish

Darn in loose ends.
Put all pieces into washing machine and wash on a high temperature to felt bag.
When pieces are dry, sew two ends of handle together, using backstitch or an edge-to-edge seam.
Pin Front to one edge of handle with right sides facing and handle seam positioned at bottom of bag; sew in place. Repeat with Back.
Using yarn A, make a thread loop on inside top edge of back: work several stitches in same place, making a loop large enough for button, then cover these threads with closely worked buttonhole stitch (see page 71).
Sew button onto the top of Front, opposite the loop.

Chequered cushion

The lacy edging on this chequered cushion cover gives
a perfect soft touch for a bedroom – or you could omit
the edging and make it in colours to suit your sofa.

Skill level
Intermediate

Techniques
• Stocking/stockinette stitch
  (page 19)
• Following a chart (pages 66–67)
• Intarsia method (pages 62–63)
• Knitting two stitches together
  (page 31)
• Yarn forward increase (page 30)
• Inserting a zip (page 92)
• Darning in ends (page 37)
• Seams (page 36)

Tools
1 pair of 5mm (UK 6) (US 8)
  knitting needles
1 pair of 6mm (UK 4) (US 10)
  knitting needles
13 bobbins
Basic equipment for finishing
  (see page 35)

Materials
Rowan Cotton Rope
6 × 50g (1¾oz) balls in Khaki,
73 **(A)**

4 × balls in String,
72 **(B)**

4 × balls in Strawberry,
74 **(C)**

Alternative Colours
Variation 1
Limeade,
65 **(A)**

Lemonade,
60 **(B)**

Calypso,
64 **(C)**

Variation 2
White,
67 **(A)**

Strawberry,
74 **(B)**

Navy,
75 **(C)**

40cm/16in zip
Cushion pad/pillow form,
40 × 40cm/16 × 16in

Tension/gauge
15 sts and 20 rows to 10cm/4in
measured over st st using 6mm
(UK 4) (US 10) needles. Change
needle size if necessary to obtain
correct tension/gauge.

Abbreviations
See page 6.

Measurements
Finished size approximately 42 × 42cm (16½ × 16½in), not
including lace edging

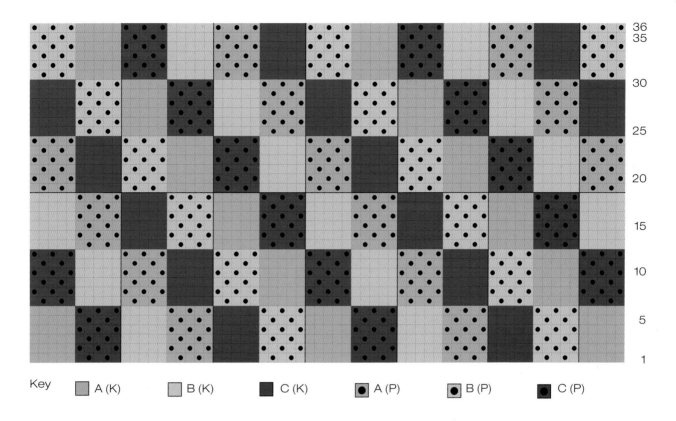

Key ☐ A (K) ☐ B (K) ■ C (K) ⊙ A (P) ⊙ B (P) ● C (P)

Notes

When changing colour always twist the yarns on the WS of your work, as explained for the intarsia method (see pages 62–63), to avoid leaving a hole.

Because the zip is inserted in the firm cast-off/bound-off edge of the cushion cover, rather than a side edge, there is no need for the selvedge recommended on page 92 for inserting a zip.

If you wish to make the back of the cover a solid colour, work as for the front but using one colour throughout. You will need 12 balls of yarn in total.

Front

Using larger needles and *yarn A, cast on 5 sts, using B cast on 5 sts, using C cast on 5 sts, rep from * until 65 sts are on the needle.

Row 1 *K5 in A, (K1, P1, K1, P1, K1) in C, K5 in B, (K1, P1, K1, P1, K1) in A, K5 in C , (K1, P1, K1, P1, K1) in B, rep from * once, K5 in A.

Cont from chart, starting on row 2, until 36 rows of chart have been worked twice, then work rows 1–12 again.

Cast/bind off in each colour.

Back

Work as for Front.

If you want a solid colour for the Back, work as for Front but using one colour throughout.

Edging (worked lengthways)

Using smaller needles and A, cast on 8 sts.

Row 1 (RS) Sl 1, K2, yf, K2tog, (yf) twice to make 2 sts, K2tog, K1. 9 sts.

Row 2 K3, P1, K2, yf, K2tog, K1.

Row 3 Sl 1, K2, yf, K2tog, K1, (yf) twice, K2tog, K1. 10 sts.

Row 4 K3, P1, K3, yf, K2tog, K1.

Row 5 Sl 1, K2, yf, K2tog, K2, (yf) twice, K2tog, K1. 11 sts.

Row 6 K3, P1, K4, yf, K2tog, K1.

Row 7 Sl 1, K2, yf, K2tog, K6.

Row 8 Cast/bind off 3 sts, K4, yf, K2tog, K1. 8 sts.

These 8 rows form the patt.

Cont in patt until edging fits around 4 sides of cushion Front, finishing with row 8.

Cast/bind off.

To finish

Press Back and Front carefully, following instructions on yarn label. Block the edging to open out lace pattern. Darn in loose ends.

Insert zip between two cast-off/bound-off edges. Open zip and sew remaining edges using backstitch or an edge-to-edge seam.

Placing edging and cushion front right side up and starting at one corner, sew on edging as closely as possible to cushion cover seam by picking up one stitch from edging then one from cushion alternately. Sew cast-on stitches to cast-off/bound-off stitches of edging.

Big blanket

Each square for this thick and cosy blanket is knitted separately – which makes it an easily portable project – and the squares are then sewn together. You can arrange the squares to suit your own taste.

Skill level
Intermediate

Techniques
- Stocking/stockinette stitch (page 19)
- Intarsia method (pages 62–63)
- Following a chart (pages 66–67)
- Seams (page 36)

Tools
1 pair of 12mm (US 17) knitting needles
7 bobbins (see page 15)
Basic equipment for finishing (see page 35)

Materials
Rowan Big Wool
3 × 100g (3½oz) balls in Wild Berry, 25 (**A**)

3 × balls in Lucky, 20 (**B**)

3 × balls in Latte, 18 (**C**)

3 × balls in Sugar Spun, 16 (**D**)

3 × balls in Ice Blue, 21 (**E**)

3 × balls in Zing, 37 (**F**)

Alternative colours
Sugar Spun, 16 (**A**)

Latte, 18 (**B**)

Ginger Snap, 39 (**C**)

Acer, 41 (**D**)

Mulberry, 42 (**E**)

Smoky, 7 (**F**)

Tension/gauge
9 sts and 11½ rows to 10cm/4in measured over st st using 12mm (US 17) needles. Change needle size if necessary to obtain correct tension/gauge.

Abbreviations
See page 6.

Notes
Each square consists of a moss/seed stitch edging around a central square of stocking/stockinette stitch. When changing colour always twist the yarns on the WS of the work, as explained for the intarsia method (see pages 62–63), to avoid leaving a hole.

Measurements
Individual square   20 × 20cm (8 × 8in)
Finished blanket   100 × 140cm (40 × 56in)

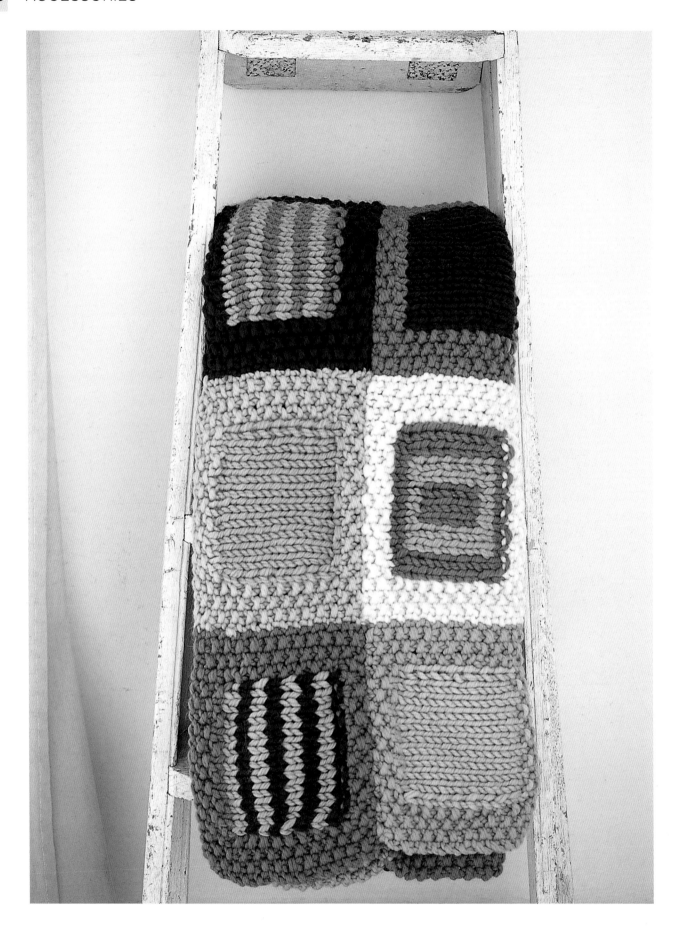

Basic square

Using yarn E, cast on 19 sts.
Row 1 K1, *P1, K1, rep from * to end.
Row 2 K1, *P1, K1, rep from * to end. These 2 rows form moss/seed st patt.
Rows 3 and 4 Rep rows 1 and 2 once more.
Row 5 K1, P1, K1, P1 in E, change to F, K11, change to E, P1, K1, P1, K1.
Row 6 K1, P1, K1, P1 in E, change to F, P11, change to E, P1, K1, P1, K1.
Rows 7–20 (Rep rows 5 and 6) 7 times.
Rows 21–24 Using E, work in moss/seed st.
Cast/bind off.
Now work each square separately, making a total of 35 squares. Follow basic square pattern, following charts for colour variations.

To finish

Arrange squares in design of your choice. Sew all squares in each short row together, using backstitch or an edge-to-edge seam (recommended for a flatter surface and a neater underside); then sew together all long rows in same way.
Darn in loose ends.

Charts for big blanket

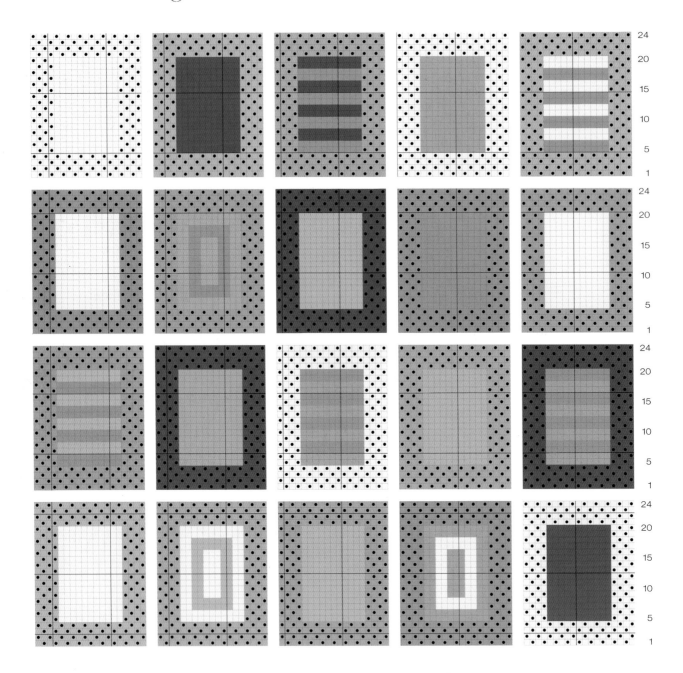

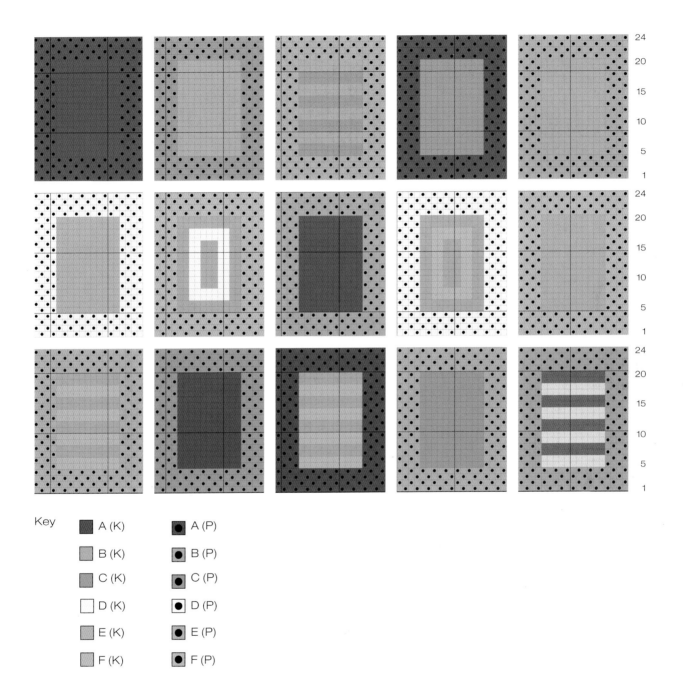

Key

A (K) A (P)
B (K) B (P)
C (K) C (P)
D (K) D (P)
E (K) E (P)
F (K) F (P)

Tote bag

This attractive little tote bag is perfect for carrying all sorts of things: a collapsible umbrella, a stuffed toy for a toddler, a gift for your hostess. The square shape makes it simple to knit, while the textured stitches add visual interest.

Skill level
Easy

Techniques
• Stocking/stockinette stitch (page 19)
• Moss/seed stitch (page 168)
• Seams (page 36)

Tools
1 pair of 3.75mm (UK 9) (US 5) knitting needles
Basic equipment for finishing (see page 35)

Materials
Jaeger Matchmaker Merino DK
1 × 50g (1¾oz) ball in Mariner, 629

Tension/gauge
24 sts and 36 rows to 10cm/4in measured over st st using 3.75mm (UK 9) (US 5) needles. Change needle size if necessary to obtain correct tension/gauge.

Abbreviations
See page 6.

Front and back (alike)
Cast on 61 sts.
Row 1 (RS) K1, *P1, K1, rep from * to end.
Row 2 Rep row 1.
These 2 rows form moss/seed st patt.
Work in moss/seed st for 10 more rows, ending with RS facing for next row.
Starting with a K row, work in st st for 5 rows, ending with WS facing for next row.
**K 3 rows.
Starting with a K row, work in st st for 5 rows, ending with WS facing for next row.

Rep from ** 9 more times.
K 3 rows, ending with RS facing for next row.
Starting with a K row, work in st st for 5 rows, ending with WS facing for next row.
Work in moss/seed st for 12 rows, ending with WS facing for next row.
Cast/bind off in moss/seed st.

Handles (make 2)
Cast on 7 sts.
Work in moss/seed st until handle measures 36cm/14in, ending with RS facing for next row.
Cast/bind off in moss/seed st.

To finish
Block pieces. Fold Bag in half with right sides together and, using backstitch for strength, sew together cast-on and row-end edges to form base and side seam. Using the photograph as a guide, sew handles to upper edges. Darn in loose ends.

Measurements
Finished size 24 × 20cm (9½ × 7¾in)

Big-ears bunny

This cute little chap is sure to become a firm family favourite and will be treasured forever. You could even knit a whole bunny brood using different-coloured yarns and give them away as special gifts. Try experimenting with the embroidery to create different facial expressions, or tying a bow tie instead of a bow.

Skill level
Intermediate

Techniques
• Garter stitch (page 19)
• Knitting two stitches together (page 31)
• Seams (page 36)
• Embroidery on knitting (pages 70–71)

Tools
1 pair of 3.25mm (UK 10) (US 3) knitting needles
1 stitch holder
1 blunt-ended yarn needle
Small pompom form (or cardboard for homemade form)
Basic equipment for finishing (see page 35)

Materials

Rowan Wool Cotton
1 × 50g (1¾oz) ball in Dream, 929

Scraps of brown yarn (for embroidery) and white (for pompom tail)
40cm/16in of narrow ribbon
Washable toy filling

Tension/gauge
24 sts and 50 rows to 10cm/4in measured over garter stitch using 3.25mm (UK 10) (US 3) needles. Change needle size if necessary to obtain correct tension/gauge.

Abbreviations
See page 6.

Measurements
Height of finished toy approximately 25cm (9¾in), including ears

Main section

First leg

Cast on 18 sts.

Row 1 K.

Row 2 K.

These 2 rows form garter st.

Cont in garter st for 34 more rows, ending with RS facing for next row.

Break yarn and leave sts on a holder.

Second leg

Cast on 18 sts.

Work in garter st for 36 rows, ending with RS facing for next row.

Join legs

Next row (RS) K 18 sts of Second Leg, then K 18 sts of First Leg. 36 sts.

Work in garter st for 36 more rows (for Body), ending with WS facing for next row.

Shape head

Next row (WS) *K2tog, K2, rep from * to end. 27 sts.

Work in garter st for 28 rows more (for Head), ending with RS facing for next row.

Cast/bind off.

Arms (alike)

Cast on 16 sts.

Work in garter st for 34 rows, ending with RS facing for next row. Cast/bind off.

Ears (alike)

Cast on 6 sts.

Work in garter st for 26 rows, ending with RS facing for next row.

Cast/bind off.

To finish

Do NOT press.

Fold Main Section in half and sew row-end edges from cast-off/bound-off edge to top of Legs to form back seam. Fold Legs in half and sew together row-end and cast-on edges to form inside leg and foot seams. Insert toy filling and sew top of Head closed. Run a gathering thread around neck decrease row, pull up tight and fasten off securely. Using photograph as a guide, fold in top corners of ears and join edges. Sew Ears to top of Head. Fold Arms in half and sew together row-end and cast-on edges to form arm and hand seams. Insert toy filling, then sew Arms to sides of Body. Using photograph as a guide, embroider face on Head using brown yarn and blunt-ended yarn needle. For eyes, work 2 cross stitches. Embroider nose by working 2 straight stitches very closely together and work mouth using straight stitches. Work one cross stitch at waist, as in photograph. Using white yarn, make a tiny pompom and attach to back seam for tail. Tie ribbon in bow around neck.

Ideal for the beginner wanting to explore patterns of their own or a wider range of designs, here is a collection of knitted swatches showing the different textures and patterns that can be achieved using various stitches. There are 40 swatches in total.

Stitch gallery

Moss/seed stitch

Multiple of 2
Row 1 (RS) *K1, P1, rep from *.
Row 2 *P1, K1, rep from *.
Rep rows 1 and 2.

Diamond seed

Multiple of 8
Row 1 (RS) *P1, K7, rep from *.
Rows 2 and 8 *K1, P5, K1, P1, rep
from *.
Rows 3 and 7 *K2, P1, K3, P1, K1, rep
from *.
Rows 4 and 6 *P2, K1, P1, K1, P3, rep
from *.
Row 5 *K4, P1, K3, rep from *.
Rep rows 1–8.

Roman stitch

Multiple of 2
Rows 1 and 3 (RS) K.
Rows 2 and 4 P.
Row 5 *K1, P1, rep from *.
Row 6 *P1, K1, rep from *.
Rep rows 1–6.

Basketweave

Multiple of 8 plus 4 extra
Row 1 (RS) K4, *P4, K4, rep from *.
Row 2 P4, *K4, P4, rep from *.
Rows 3 and 4 Rep rows 1 and 2.
Rows 5 and 7 Rep row 2.
Rows 6 and 8 Rep row 1.
Rep rows 1–8.

Single twisted rib

Multiple of 2
Row 1 (RS) *K1 tbl, P1, rep from *.
Row 2 Rep row 1.
Rep rows 1 and 2.

Embossed chevron

Multiple of 12
Row 1 (RS) *K3, P5, K3, P1, rep from *.
Row 2 and every alternate row K the K sts and P the P sts as they appear.
Row 3 P1, *K3, P3, rep from * to last 5 sts, K3, P2.
Row 5 P2, *K3, P1, K3, P5, rep from * to last 10 sts, K3, P1, K3, P3.
Row 7 *P3, K5, P3, K1, rep from *.
Row 9 K1, *P3, K3, rep from * to last 5 sts, P3, K2.
Row 11 K2, *P3, K1, P3, K5, rep from * ending last rep K3.
Row 12 Rep row 2.
Rep rows 1–12.

Honeycomb slipstitch

Multiple of 2 plus 1 extra
Row 1 (RS) P1, *sl 1 purlwise, P1, rep from *.
Rows 2 and 4 P.
Row 3 P2, *sl 1 purlwise, P1, rep from * to last st, P1.
Rep rows 1–4.

Nut pattern

Multiple of 4
Row 1 (RS) *P3, (K1, yf, K1) into next st, rep from *.
Rows 2 and 3 *P3, K3, rep from *.
Row 4 *P3tog, K3, rep from *.
Row 5 P.
Row 6 K.
Row 7 *P1, (K1, yf, K1) into next st, P2, rep from *.
Row 8 K2, *P3, K3, rep from * to last 4 sts, P3, K1.
Row 9 P1, *K3, P3, rep from * to last 5 sts, K3, P2.
Row 10 K2, *P3tog, K3, rep from * to last 4 sts, P3tog, K1.
Row 11 P.
Row 12 K.
Rep rows 1–12.

Fisherman's rib

Multiple of 2
Row 1 P.
Row 2 *P1, K next st in the row below,
rep from * to last 2 sts, P2.
Rep row 2 throughout.

Leaf pattern

Multiple of 24 plus 1 extra
Note 'K up 1': Pick up a stitch (see page 33).
Row 1 (RS) K1, *K up 1, sl 1, K1, psso, K4, K2tog,
K3, K up 1, K1, K up 1, K3, sl 1, K1, psso, K4, K2tog,
K up 1, K1, rep from *.
Row 2 and every alternate row P.
Row 3 K1, *K up 1, K1, sl 1, K1, psso, K2, K2tog, K4,
K up 1, K1, K up 1, K4, sl 1, K1, psso, K2, K2tog, K1,
K up 1, K1, rep from *.
Row 5 K1, *K up 1, K2, sl 1, K1, psso, K2 tog, K5,
K up 1, K1, K up 1, K5, sl 1, K1, psso, K2tog, K2,
K up 1, K1, rep from *.
Row 7 K1, *K up 1, K3, sl 1, K1, psso, K4, K2tog,
K up 1, K1, K up 1, sl 1, K1, psso, K4, K2tog, K3,
K up 1, K1, rep from *.
Row 9 K1, *K up 1, K4, sl 1, K1, psso, K2, K2tog, K1,
K up 1, K1, K up 1, K1, sl 1, K1, psso, K2, K2tog, K4,
K up 1, K1, rep from *.
Row 11 K1, *K up 1, K5, sl 1, K1, psso, K2tog, K2,
K up 1, K1, K up 1, K2, sl 1, K1, psso, K2tog, K5,
K up 1, K1, rep from *.
Row 12 Rep row 2.
Rep rows 1–12.

Quatrefoil eyelet

Multiple of 8
Row 1 and every alternate row (WS) P.
Row 2 K.
Row 4 K3, *yf, sl 1, K1, psso, K6, rep from *ending last rep K3 instead of K6.
Row 6 K1, *K2 tog, yf, K1, yf, sl 1, K1, psso, K3, rep from * ending last rep K2 instead of K3.
Row 8 Rep row 4.
Row 10 K.
Row 12 K7, *yf, sl 1, K1, psso, K6, rep from * to last st, K1.
Row 14 K5, *K2tog, yf, K1, yf, sl 1, K1, psso, K3, rep from * to last 3 sts, K3.
Row 16 Rep row 12.
Rep rows 1–16.

Vandyke stitch

Multiple of 10
Row 1 (RS) *Yf, sl 1, K1, psso, K8, rep from *.
Row 2 and every alternate row P.
Row 3 *K1, yf, sl 1, K1, psso, K5, K2tog, yf, rep from * ending last rep K2 not K2tog, yf.
Row 5 *K2, yf, sl 1, K1, psso, K3, K2tog, yf, K1, rep from *.
Row 7 *K5, yf, sl 1, K1, psso, K3, rep from *.
Row 9 *K3, K2tog, yf, K1, yf, sl 1, K1, psso, K2, rep from *.
Row 11 *K2, K2tog, yf, K3, yf, sl 1, K1, psso, K1, rep from *.
Row 12 P.
Rep rows 1–12.

Fern lace

Multiple of 10 plus 1 extra
Row 1 and every alternate row (WS) P.
Row 2 K3, *K2 tog, yf, K1, yf, sl 1, K1, psso, K5, rep from * ending last rep K3.
Row 4 K2, *K2 tog, (K1, yf) twice, K1, sl 1, K1, psso, K3, rep from * ending last rep K2.
Row 6 K1, *K2 tog, K2, yf, K1, yf, K2, sl 1, K1, psso, K1, rep from *.
Row 8 K2 tog, *K3, yf, K1, yf, K3, sl 1, K2tog, psso, rep from * to last 9 sts, K3, yf, K1, yf, K3, sl 1, K1, psso.
Row 10 K1, *yf, sl 1, K1, psso, K5, K2tog, yf, K1, rep from *.
Row 12 K1, *yf, K1, sl 1, K1, psso, K3, K2tog, K1, yf, K1, rep from *.
Row 14 K1, *yf, K2, sl 1, K1, psso, K1, K2tog, K2, yf, K1, rep from *.
Row 16 K1, *yf, K3, sl 1, K2tog, psso, K3, yf, K1, rep from *.
Rep rows 1–16.

Curving lattice lace

Multiple of 13 plus 2 extra
Row 1 (RS) K1, *K2, sl 1, K1, psso, K4, K2tog, K2, yf, K1, yf, rep from * to last st, K1.
Row 2 and every alternate row P.
Row 3 K1, *yf, K2, sl 1, K1, psso, K2, K2tog, K2, yf, K3, rep from * to last st, K1.
Row 5 K1, *K1, yf, K2, sl 1, K1, psso, K2tog, K2, yf, K4, rep from * to last st, K1.
Row 7 K1,*yf, K1, yf, K2, sl 1, K1, psso, K4, K2tog, K2, rep from * to last st, K1.
Row 9 K1, *K3, yf, K2, sl 1, K1, psso, K2, K2tog, K2, yf, rep from * to last st, Kl.
Row 11 K1, * K4, yf, K2, sl 1, K1, psso, K2tog, K2, yf, K1, rep from * to last st, K1.
Row 12 P.
Rep rows 1–12.

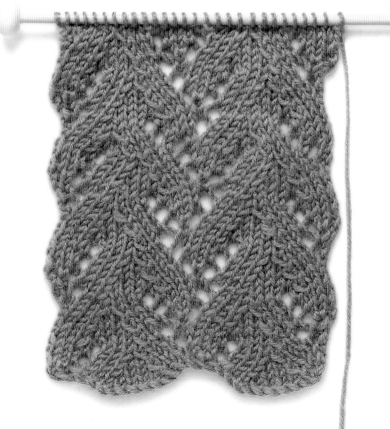

Gull cable

Worked over 7 sts
Row 1 RS K7.
Row 2 P7.
Row 3 Sl 2 sts onto cable needle and hold at back of work, K1 then K2 from cable needle, K1, sl 1 st onto cable needle and hold at front of work, K2 then K1 from cable needle.
Row 4 P7.
Rep rows 1–4.

Trellis cables

Multiple of 6 plus 2 extra
Note 'C3B': sl next 2 sts onto cable needle and hold at back of work, K1, P2 from cable needle.
'C3F': sl next st onto cable needle and hold at front of work, P2, K1 from cable needle.
Rows 1 and 3 (RS) P3, *K2, P4, rep from * to last 5 sts, K2, P3.
Rows 2 and 4 K3, *P2, K4, rep from * to last 5 sts, P2, K3.
Row 5 P1, *C3B, C3F, rep from * to last st, P1.
Rows 6, 8 and 10 K1, P1, *K4, P2, rep from * to last 6 sts, K4, P1, K1.
Rows 7 and 9 P1, K1, *P4, K2, rep from * to last 6 sts, P4, K1, P1.
Row 11 P1, *C3F, C3B, rep from * to last st, P1.
Row 12 Rep row 2.
Rep rows 1–12.

Interlaced cable

Worked over 13 sts

Note 'Cr3F': sl next 2 sts onto cable needle and hold at front of work, P1, then K2 from cable needle. 'Cr3B': sl next st onto cable needle and hold at back of work, K2, then P1 from cable needle.

Row 1 (WS) P2, K2, P2, K1, P2, K2, P2.

Row 2 K2, P2, sl next 3 sts onto cable needle and hold at back of work, K2, sl P st from cable needle back onto LH needle and P it, K2 from cable needle, P2, K2.

Row 3 Rep row 1.

Row 4 Cr3F, Cr3B, P1, Cr3F, Cr3B.

Row 5 K1, P4, K3, P4, K1.

Row 6 P1, C4B, P3, C4F, P1.

Row 7 Rep row 5.

Row 8 Cr3B, Cr3F, P1, Cr3B, Cr3F.

Row 9 Rep row 1.

Row 10 K2, P2, sl next 3 sts onto cable needle and hold at front of work, K2, sl P st from cable needle back onto LH needle and P it, K2 from cable needle, P2, K2.

Rows 11–16 Rep rows 3–8.

Rep rows 1–16.

Eyelet and bobble pattern

Multiple of 9 plus 4 extra

Row 1 (RS) K1, *(yf, sl 1, K1, psso) twice, K5, rep from * to last 3 sts, K3.

Row 2 and every alternate row P.

Row 3 K2, *(yf, sl 1, K1, psso) twice, K5, rep from * to last 2 sts, K2.

Row 5 K3, *(yf, sl 1, K1, psso) twice, K5, rep from * to last st, K1.

Row 7 K4, *(yf, sl 1, K1, psso) twice, K2, **K into front and back of st twice, turn, P4, turn, K4, pass 2nd, 3rd and 4th sts over first st **, K2, rep from *.

Row 9 K3, *(K2 tog, yf) twice, K5, rep from * to last st, K1.

Row 11 K2, *(K2 tog, yf) twice, K5, rep from * to last 2 sts, K2.

Row 13 K1, *(K2 tog, yf) twice, K5, rep from * to last 3 sts, K3.

Row 15 *(K2 tog, yf) twice, K2, work from ** to ** of row 7, K2, rep from * to last 4 sts, K4.

Row 16 P.

Rep rows 1–16.

Simple bobble stitch

Multiple of 6 plus 1 extra
Row 1 (RS) *K3, **K into front, back and front of next st, turn and K the 3 sts, turn and P the 3 sts, turn and K the 3 sts, turn and pass the 2nd st over the first st, pass the 3rd st over the first st, slip st onto RH needle **, K2, rep from * to last st, K1.
Rows 2, 4 and 6 P.
Rows 3 and 5 K.
Row 7 *Work from ** to ** of row 1, K5, rep from * to last st, work from ** to **.
Rows 8 and 10 P.
Rows 9 and 11 K.
Row 12 P.
Rep rows 1–12.

Nosegay pattern

Worked over 16 sts
Note 'Cr2B': sl next st onto cable needle and hold at back of work, K1, then P1 from cable needle. 'Cr2F': sl next st onto cable needle and hold at front of work, P1, then K1 from cable needle.
'Make bobble': (K1, yf, K1, yf, K1) into next st, turn, P5, turn, K5, turn, P2tog, P1, P2tog, turn, sl 1, K2tog, psso.
Row 1 (WS) K7, P2, K7.
Row 2 P6, C2B, C2F, P6.
Row 3 K5, Cr2F, P2, Cr2B, K5.
Row 4 P4, Cr2B, C2B, C2F, Cr2F, P4.
Row 5 K3, Cr2F, K1, P4, K1, Cr2B, K3.
Row 6 P2, Cr2B, P1, Cr2B, K2, Cr2F, P1, Cr2F, P2.
Row 7 (K2 P1) twice, K1, P2, K1, (P1, K2) twice.
Row 8 P2, make bobble, P1, Cr2B, P1, K2, P1, Cr2F, P1, make bobble, P2.
Row 9 K4, P1, K2, P2, K2, P1, K4.
Row 10 P4, make bobble, P2, K2, P2, make bobble, P4.
Rep rows 1–10.

Crossed-stitch rib

Multiple of 3 plus 1 extra

Note 'Tw2R': K into front of 2nd st, K into front of first st, sl both sts off LH needle.

Row 1 (RS) P1, *Tw2R, P1, rep from *.

Row 2 K1,*P2, K1, rep from *.

Rep rows 1 and 2.

Linked check pattern

Multiple of 10

Note 'Tw2R': K into front of 2nd st, then K into front of first st, sl both sts off LH needle.

'Tw2PL': P into 2nd st, sl this st over first st and off needle, P first st tbl. (This technique varies from the Tw2PL shown on page 41.)

Row 1 (RS) *K4, P2, Tw2R, P2, rep from *.

Row 2 *K2, Tw2PL, K2, P4, rep from *.

Rows 3 and 5 Rep row 1.

Rows 4 and 6 Rep row 2.

Row 7 *P1, Tw2R, P2, K4, P1, rep from *.

Row 8 *K1, P4, K2, Tw2PL, K1, rep from *.

Rows 9 and 11 Rep row 7.

Rows 10 and 12 Rep row 8.

Rep rows 1–12.

Maltese cross medallion

Cast on 8 sts. (In this example, a crocheted chain [see page 53] has been used as the foundation.) Arrange the sts evenly on 4 needles, and use a fifth for the knitting.

Round 1 K every st tbl.
Round 2 *K1, yf, rep from *. 16 sts.
Round 3 and every alternate round K.
Round 4 K1, *yf, K2, rep from * to last st, yf, K1. 24 sts.
Round 6 K2, *yf, K2, yf, K4, rep from * ending last rep K2 instead of K4. 32 sts. Cont in this way, inc to either side of the 2 centre sts on each needle on alternate rounds, until the medallion is the required size. Cast/bind off loosely.
For a solid medallion work as above, but work a bar inc or a 'make 1' inc to either side of the centre 2 sts (see pages 28 and 29).

Swirl hexagon

Cast on 12 sts. (A knitted foundation has been used for this example.) Divide the sts evenly onto 3 needles, and K with a fourth.

Round 1 K every st tbl.
Round 2 *Yf, K2, rep from *. 18 sts.
Round 3 and every alternate round K.
Round 4 *Yf, K3, rep from *. 24 sts.
Round 6 *'Yf, K4, rep from *. 30 sts.
Cont in this way until hexagon is the required size.
Cast/bind off loosely.

Circular target medallion

Cast on 8 sts. (In this example, a crocheted chain [see page 53] has been used as the foundation.) Arrange the sts evenly on 4 needles, and use a fifth for the knitting.

Round 1 K every st tbl.

Round 2 *Yf, K1, rep from *. 16 sts.

Rounds 3, 4 and 5 K.

Round 6 *Yf, K1, rep from *. 32 sts.

Rounds 7–11 K.

Round 12 *Yf, K1, rep from *. 64 sts.

Rounds 13–19 K.

The example shown has been worked up to round 14, then cast/bind off and finished with a crocheted edging. To make the medallion larger, cont as follows:

Round 20 *Yf, K2, rep from *. 96 sts.

Rounds 21–25 K.

Round 26 *Yf, K3, rep from *. 128 sts.

Rounds 25–31 K.

Round 32 *Yf, K4, rep from *. 160 sts.

Cont in this way, working 5 plain rounds between every inc round and inc 32 sts on every subsequent inc round, spacing them evenly (for example, round 38 will have 5 K sts between the inc).

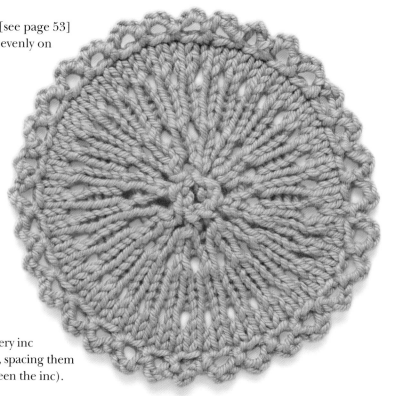

Three-colour tweed

Multiple of 3 plus 1 extra

Note Colour A = yellow, Colour B = dark blue, Colour C = pale blue.

Row 1 (WS) With A, K.

Row 2 With B, K3, *sl 1 wyb, K2, rep from * to last st, K1.

Row 3 With B, K3, *sl 1 wyf, K2, rep from * to last st, K1.

Row 4 With C, *K2, sl 1 wyb, rep from * to last st, K1.

Row 5 With C, K1, *sl 1 wyf, K2, rep from *.

Row 6 With A, K1, *sl 1 wyb, K2, rep from *.

Row 7 With A, *K2, sl 1 wyf, rep from * to last st, K1.

Rep rows 2 to 7.

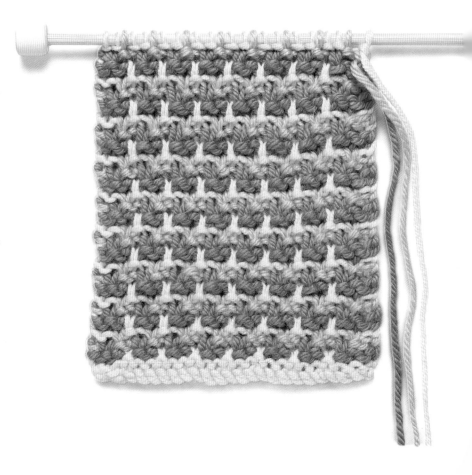

Linked stripe pattern

Multiple of 4
Note Colour A = yellow, Colour B = turquoise.
Rows 1 , 2, 5 and 6 (RS) With A, K.
Rows 3 and 7 With B, K1, *sl 2 wyb, K2, rep from * ending sl 2, K1.
Rows 4 and 8 With B, P1, *sl 2 wyf, P2, rep from * ending sl 2, P1.
Rows 9, 10, 13 and 14 With B, K.
Rows 11 and 15 With A, K1, *sl 2 wyb, K2, rep from * ending sl 2, K1.
Rows 12 and 16 With A, P1, *sl 2 wyf, P2, rep from * ending sl 2, P1.
Rep rows 1–16.

Multicoloured stripes

Multiple of 4 plus 3 extra
Note Colour A = yellow, Colour B = turquoise, Colour C = blue, Colour D = pink.
Row 1 (WS) With A, P.
Row 2 With B, K2, *sl 1 wyb, K1, rep from * to last st, K1,
Row 3 With B, P2, *sl 1 wyf, P1, rep from * to last st, P1.
Row 4 With C, K1, *sl 1 wyb, K1, rep from *.
Row 5 With C, P.
Row 6 With D. K1, *sl 1 wyb, K3, rep from * to last 2 sts, sl 1 wyb, K1.
Row 7 With D, P1, *sl 1 wyf, P3, rep from * to last 2 sts, sl 1 wyf, P1.
Row 8 With B, K2, *sl 3 wyb, K1, rep from * to last st, K1.
Row 9 With B, *P3, sl 1 wyf, rep from * to last 3 sts, P3.
Row 10 With A, K1, *sl 1 wyb, K3, rep from * to last 2 sts, sl 1 wyb, K1.
Rep rows 1–10.

Argyle – 14 rows/16 stitches

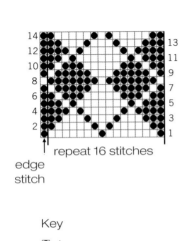

repeat 16 stitches

edge
stitch

Key
● A
□ B

Diamond spot – 6 rows/8 stitches

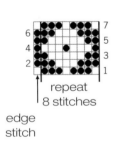

repeat
8 stitches

edge
stitch

Key
● A
□ B

Work rows 1 to 7, repeat rows 2 to 7.

Greek key – 20 rows/16 stitches

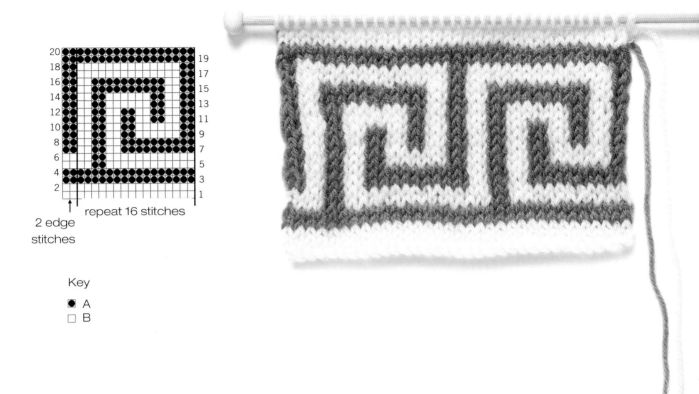

20
18
16
14
12
10
8
6
4
2

19
17
15
13
11
9
7
5
3
1

↑ 2 edge stitches

repeat 16 stitches

Key
● A
☐ B

Cross pattern

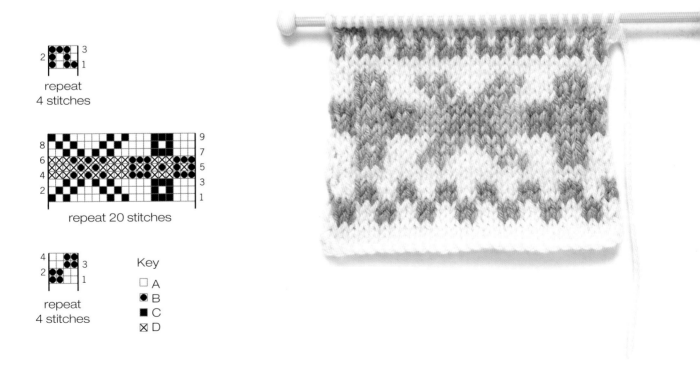

2
3
1

repeat
4 stitches

8
6
4
2

9
7
5
3
1

repeat 20 stitches

4
2
3
1

repeat
4 stitches

Key
☐ A
● B
■ C
☒ D

Entwined hearts

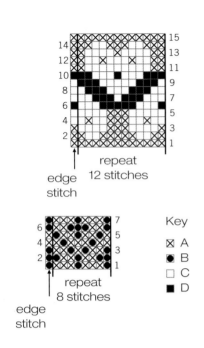

edge
stitch

repeat
12 stitches

edge
stitch

repeat
8 stitches

Key
⊠ A
● B
☐ C
■ D

Snowflake

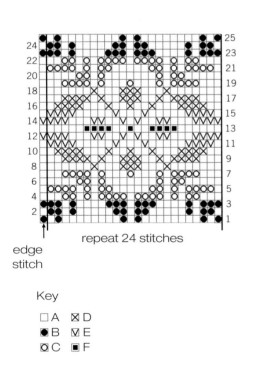

edge
stitch

repeat 24 stitches

Key
☐ A ⊠ D
● B Ⅴ E
◉ C ■ F

Leaf edging

This edging is worked sideways. Cast on 8 sts.
Row 1 (RS) K5, yf, K1, yf, K2.
Row 2 P6, K into front and back of next st, K3.
Row 3 K4, P1, K2, yf, K1, yf, K3.
Row 4 P8, K into front and back of next st, K4.
Row 5 K4, P2, K3, yf, K1, yf, K4.
Row 6 P10, K into front and back of next st, K5.
Row 7 K4, P3, K4, yf, K1, yf, K5.
Row 8 P12, K into front and back of next st, K6.
Row 9 K4, P4, sl 1, K1, psso, K7, K2 tog, K1.
Row 10 P10, K into front and back of next st, K7.
Row 11 K4, P5, sl 1, K1, psso, K5, K2 tog, K1.
Row 12 P8, K into front and back of next st, K2, P1, K5.
Row 13 K4, P1, K1, P4, sl 1, K1, psso, K3, K2 tog, K1.
Row 14 P6, K into front and back of next st, K3, P1, K5.
Row 15 K4, P1, K1, P5, sl 1, K1, psso, K1, K2 tog, K1.
Row 16 P4, K into front and back of next st, K4, P1, K5.
Row 17 K4, P1, K1, P6, sl 1, K2 tog, psso, K1.
Row 18 P2tog, cast/bind off 5 sts knitwise using P2tog to cast/bind off first st, P3, K4.
8 sts remain.
Rep rows 1–18.

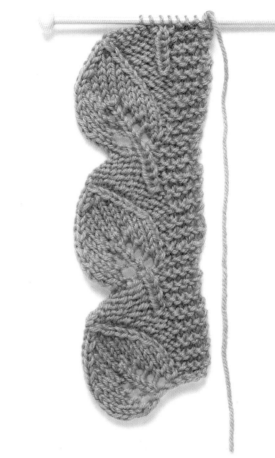

Faggot and scallop edging

This edging is worked sideways. Cast on 13 sts.
Row 1 K7, yf, sl 1, K1, psso, yf, K4.
Row 2 K2, P10, K2.
Row 3 K6, (yf, sl 1, K1, psso) twice, yf, K4.
Row 4 K2, P11, K2.
Row 5 K5, (yf, sl 1, K1, psso) 3 times, yf, K4.
Row 6 K2, P12, K2.
Row 7 K4, (yf, sl 1, K1, psso) 4 times, yf, K4.
Row 8 K2, P13, K2.
Row 9 K3, (yf, sl 1, K1, psso) 5 times, yf, K4.
Row 10 K2, P14, K2.
Row 11 K4, (yf, sl 1, K1, psso) 5 times, K2 tog, K2.
Row 12 K2, P13, K2.
Row 13 K5, (yf, sl 1, K1, psso) 4 times, K2 tog, K2.
Row 14 K2, P12, K2.
Row 15 K6, (yf, sl 1, K1, psso) 3 times, K2 tog, K2.
Row 16 K2, P11, K2
Row 17 K7, (yf, sl 1, K1, psso) twice, K2 tog, K2.
Row 18 K2, P10, K2.
Row 19 K8, yf, sl 1, K1, psso, K2 tog, K2.
Row 20 K2, P9, K2.
Rep rows 1–20.

Godmother's edging

This edging is worked sideways.
Cast on 20 sts.
Row 1 (WS) K.
Row 2 Sl 1, K3, (yf, K2 tog) 7 times, yf, K2.
Rows 3, 5, 7 and 9 K.
Row 4 Sl 1, K6, (yf, K2 tog) 6 times, yf, K2.
Row 6 Sl 1, K9, (yf, K2 tog) 5 times, yf, K2.
Row 8 Sl 1, K12, (yf, K2 tog) 4 times, yf, K2.
Row 10 Sl 1, K23.
Row 11 Cast/bind off 4 sts, K19.
20 sts remain.
Rep rows 2–11.

Zigzag ribbon pattern

Multiple of 11 plus 2
Row 1 (RS) K1, *P1, K10, rep from * to
last st, K1.
Row 2 K1, *P9, K2, rep from * to last st, K1.
Row 3 K1, *P3, K8, rep from * to last st, K1.
Row 4 K1, *P7, K4, rep from * to last st, K1.
Row 5 K1, *P5, K6, rep from * to last st, K1.
Rows 6 and 7 Rep row 5.
Row 8 Rep row 4.
Row 9 Rep row 3.
Row 10 Rep row 2.
Row 11 Rep row 1.
Row 12 K1, *K1, P10, rep from * to last st, K1.
Row 13 K1, *K9, P2, rep from * to last st, K1.
Row 14 K1, *K3, P8, rep from * to last st, K1.
Row 15 K1, *K7, P4, rep from * to last st, K1.
Row 16 K1, *K5, P6, rep from * to last st, K1.
Rows 17 and 18 As Row 16.
Row 19 Rep row 15.
Row 20 Rep row 14.
Row 21 Rep row 13.
Row 22 Rep row 12.
Rep rows 1–22.

Entrelacs pattern

Multiple of 6

Note Colour A = fawn, Colour B = brown, Colour C = beige.

Join in and break off yarns where necessary.

Foundation row (base triangles) With A, *P2, turn and K2, turn and P3, turn and K3, turn and P4, turn and K4, turn and P5, turn and K5, turn and P6, rep from *.

Cont in stripe sequence of 1 row in B, 1 row in C, and 1 row in A, as follows:

Row 1 (RS) K2, turn and P2, turn and inc in first st, sl 1, K1, psso, turn and P3, turn and inc in first st, K1, sl 1, K1, psso, turn and P4, turn and inc in first st, K2, sl 1, K1, psso, turn and P5, turn and inc in first st, K3, sl 1, K1, psso (edge triangle complete), then cont as follows: *pick up and K 6 sts down side edge of same section of previous row; working across these sts and next 6 sts on LH needle, cont as follows: (turn and P6, turn and K5, sl 1, K1, psso) 6 times, rep from * to last section, pick up and K 6 sts down side edge of last section, turn and P2tog, P4, turn and K5, turn and P2tog, P3, turn and K4, turn and P2tog, P2, turn and K3, turn and P2tog, P1, turn and K2, turn and P2tog. Fasten off.

Row 2 *With WS facing, pick up and P 6 sts down side edge of first section of previous row and working across these sts, and next 6 sts on LH needle, cont as follows: (turn and K6, turn and P5, P2tog) 6 times, rep from *.

Keeping stripe sequence correct, rep rows 1 and 2 for the required depth, ending with row 1.

Next row (finishing row) *With WS facing, pick up and P 6 sts down side edge of first section of previous row. Working across these sts and next 6 sts on LH needle, cont as follows: turn and K6, turn and P2tog, P3, P2tog, turn and K5, turn and P2tog, P2, P2tog, turn and K4, turn and P2tog, P1, P3tog, turn and K3, turn and P2tog, P3tog turn and K2, turn and P2tog. Fasten off.

Rep from *.

Candle flames

Multiple of 12 plus 2 extra

Note In this pattern the number of stitches varies from row to row. Accurate count of stitchess may be made on row 12 or row 24.

Row 1 (RS) *P2, yon, K1, yrn, P2, K2, K2tog, K3, rep from * to last 2 sts, P2.

Row 2 *K2, P6, K2, P3, rep from * to last 2 sts, K2.

Row 3 *P2, K1, (yf, K1) twice, P2, K2, K2tog, K2, rep from * to last 2 sts, P2.

Row 4 *(K2, P5) twice, rep from * to last 2 sts, K2.

Row 5 *P2, K2, yf, K1, yf, K2, P2, K2, K2tog, K1, rep from * to last 2 sts, P2.

Row 6 *K2, P4, K2, P7, rep from * to last 2 sts, K2.

Row 7 *P2, K3, yf, K1, yf, K3, P2, K2, K2tog, rep from * to last 2 sts, P2.

Row 8 *K2, P3, K2, P9, rep from * to last 2 sts, K2.

Row 9 *P2, K2, K2 tog, K5, P2, K1, K2tog, rep from * to last 2 sts, P2.

Row 10 *K2, P2, K2, P8, rep from * to last 2 sts, K2.

Row 11 *P2, K2, K2 tog, K4, P2, K2tog, rep from * to last 2 sts, P2.

Row 12 *K2, P1, K2, P7, rep from * to last 2 sts, K2.

Row 13 *P2, K2, K2tog, K3, P2, yon, K1, yrn, rep from * to last 2 sts, P2.

Row 14 *K2, P3, K2, P6, rep from * to last 2 sts, K2.

Row 15 *P2, K2, K2tog, K2, P2, (K1, yf) twice, K1, rep from * to last 2 sts, P2.

Row 16 *(K2, P5) twice, rep from * to last 2 sts, K2.

Row 17 *P2, K2, K2tog, K1, P2, K2, yf, K1, yf, K2, rep from * to last 2 sts, P2.

Row 18 *K2, P7, K2, P4, rep from * to last 2 sts, K2.

Row 19 *P2, K2, K2tog, P2, K3, yf, K1, yf, K3, rep from * to last 2 sts, P2.

Row 20 *K2, P9, K2, P3, rep from * to last 2 sts, K2.

Row 21 *P2, K1, K2 tog, P2, K2, K2 tog, K5, rep from * to last 2 sts, P2.

Row 22 *K2, P8, K2, P2, rep from * to last 2 sts, K2.

Row 23 *P2, K2 tog, P2, K2, K2tog, K4, rep from * to last 2 sts, P2.

Row 24 *K2, P7, K2, P1, rep from * to last 2 sts, K2. Rep rows 1–24.

Needle sizes

A commercial knitting pattern will specify the size(s) of needles recommended for achieving the stated tension. However, if you are making some experimental tension swatches, perhaps with a view to designing an original garment, you may find the following guidelines helpful. Bear in mind that the recommended size for a given weight of yarn is just a starting point; you may wish to move up or down one or two sizes in order to achieve the best effect with the yarn and stitch pattern you are using.

Yarn / Needle size

Yarn	Needle size
2-ply	2 mm
3-ply	2¾ mm
4-ply	3 mm
Double knitting	4 mm
Aran	5 mm
Chunky	6 mm
Extra-chunky	9 mm

Equivalent needle sizes

This chart shows you how the different knitting needle-size systems compare.

UK	Metric	US
14	2 mm	0
13	2.25 mm	1
12	2.75 mm	2
11	3 mm	–
10	3.25 mm	3
–	3.5 mm	4
9	3.75 mm	5
8	4 mm	6
7	4.5 mm	7
6	5 mm	8
5	5.5 mm	9
4	6 mm	10
3	6.5 mm	10½
2	7 mm	10½
1	7.5 mm	11
0	8 mm	11
000	9 mm	13
0000	10 mm	15
–	11 mm	16
–	12 mm	17

Index

Acknowledgements

Picture acknowledgements

Commissioned photography © **Octopus Publishing Group**/Sandra Lane.

All other photography © **Octopus Publishing Group Limited**/Adrian Pope 72; /Andy Komorowski 1, 12, 18, 19, 24, 25, 27, 33, 40, 45, 57, 60, 61, 64, 66, 67, 77, 80, 82, 166, 170, 171,172, 173, 174, 175, 176, 177, 178, 179, 180, 181, 182, 183, 184, 185, 186, 187, 188; /Janine Hosegood 14, 74, 75; /Joey Toller 98, 99, 116, 117, 119, 124, 132, 133, 162, 163, 164, 165; /Vanessa Davies 2, 4, 6, 8, 11, 12, 15, 22, 38, 48, 58, 68, 71, 78.

Executive Editor **Katy Denny**
Senior Editor **Lisa John**
Design Manager **Tokiko Morishima**
Designer **Ben Cracknell Studios**
Photographer **Sandra Lane**
Illustrator **Kuo Kang Chen**
Pattern Checker **Sue Horan**
Picture Library Assistant **Ciaran O'Reilly**
Senior Production Controller **Manjit Sihra**